"This accessible guide is an invaluable resource for both individuals and clinicians exploring the transformative potential of psychedelics. By emphasizing openness, curiosity, and embodied integration, Nielson and Gorman provide a useful pathway for those seeking to harness the potential of psychedelic experiences, while maintaining a grounded, ethical, and evidence-based perspective. Striking the right balance between scientific rigor and compassionate care, this is a must-read for those exploring psychedelics."

—**Steven C. Hayes, PhD,** Nevada Foundation Professor in the department of psychology
at the University of Nevada, Reno; and author of *A Liberated Mind*

"*The Psychedelic Therapy Workbook* is the first book I've seen that offers a comprehensive guide for the journey, and the practitioner. These practical tools provide direction, explanations and solid advice for anyone interested in psychedelic therapy. I will need many copies of this workbook in my office to pass out to anyone and everyone ready to do this work."

—**Tammy Nelson, PhD,** director of the Integrative Sex Therapy Institute, and author
of *Open Monogamy*

"This invaluable workbook is a masterful contribution at a crucial time in the psychedelic renaissance. Elizabeth Nielson and Ingmar Gorman's profound insights are grounded in their pioneering clinical research with MDMA, psilocybin, and ketamine; in their studies of the scientific literature; in their psychedelic harm reduction work; in their personal experiences; and in their work as teachers of therapists. This is an ideal textbook for a new generation."

—**Rick Doblin, PhD,** founder and president of the Multidisciplinary Association
for Psychedelic Studies (MAPS)

T0355983

THE

# PSYCHEDELIC THERAPY

WORKBOOK

**Harm Reduction Techniques for Integrating Psychedelics
in Therapy and Personal Growth**

**ELIZABETH NIELSON, PhD
INGMAR GORMAN, PhD**

New Harbinger Publications, Inc.

## Publisher's Note

NEW HARBINGER PUBLICATIONS is a registered trademark of New Harbinger Publications, Inc.

New Harbinger Publications is an employee-owned company.

Copyright © 2025 by Elizabeth Nielson and Ingmar Gorman
New Harbinger Publications, Inc.
5720 Shattuck Avenue
Oakland, CA 94609
www.newharbinger.com

Cover design by Sara Christian

Acquired by Jed Bickman

Edited by Jody Bower

Library of Congress Cataloging-in-Publication Data on file

Printed in the United States of America

27    26    25

10    9    8    7    6    5    4    3    2    1                    First Printing

This book is dedicated to our patients who trusted us with their stories
and struggles, inspiring and requiring new and creative approaches to their care.

# Contents

# Foreword

Although I certainly had no idea at the time, my first experience with a healing circle happened when I was a teenager, passing a joint around in the woods outside a school dance. As our small group gradually entered into altered states, we talked about our lives; we compared notes, and sometimes it got heavy. Mostly, I'm happy to report, it was lightened with long peals of laughter.

As youngsters, our formal drug education was minimal, and there was much we didn't know about the importance of set and setting. Certainly we'd never heard of "integration" or "harm reduction."

Some of us had "bad trips," whether due to the environment of the trip or to encountering difficult unconscious material with no understanding or support. Others, in an effort at inner exploration, ingested counterfeit substitutions, ending up on a journey they hadn't meant to take.

I was one of those others. Now, as an adult psychiatrist, I have devoted my career to not just compassionate care but harm reduction. This means drug education, helping to assure safety in both clinical research and "underground" sessions, and working to enable equitable access to health care.

Psychedelics have been around for millennia, perhaps helping to shape our physical evolution (in something called "the stoned ape" hypothesis), but definitely sparking our cultural revolutions, such as the Summer of Love in 1967. Sadly the summer of 2024 (the year this foreword is being written) was anything but. We are now in a precarious piece in the timeline. The psychedelic community was dealt a blow in June and then in August, and many of us are just starting to pick up the pieces this fall. Not only will FDA approval of MDMA-assisted therapy be deferred for several years at least, but it now seems that approval for psilocybin treatments may also be delayed.

I've spent months moving in and out of grief for the millions of traumatized people who've been patiently waiting for treatment and the thousands of clinicians who have been trained to help them.

Unfortunately, because the machinery of government is lagging behind clinicians and clients, many of us must wait. And of course, those waiting to be healed, and to do the healing, are growing impatient.

With the demand for treatment growing, and a safe, regulated supply nearly nonexistent, the stakes have never been higher for people to take matters into their own hands when it comes to healing with psychedelic therapies. But it's not all bad news. On the other hand, the National Institute for Drug Abuse just agreed to fund an NYU-based study of psilocybin to treat opiate use disorder, totaling fifteen million dollars over five years. And the VA health care delivery system (our nation's largest) seems willing and able to pick up the torch on MDMA/midomafetamine research and quite possibly development, so the end is not yet nigh.

Just as the foundation of harm reduction is education, the foundation of safe psychedelic use lies in integration. The Psychedelic Harm Reduction and Integration Model that is elaborated in this book is the key to maintaining safety as we wait for FDA approval. This workbook offers you information that will stick, and helps you make sense of your own agenda for psychedelic use. You will reflect on your values and beliefs, assess your own set and setting through exercises, and home in on your intentions prior to the experience. You will get to read from participants in psychedelic trials, and as you progress through this workbook, you will easily learn the chemical structure, pharmacology, effects, and legal status of all the medicines, whether plant-based, animal, fungal, or synthetic.

It's a lot, and you deserve every bit of this delicious data.

Ultimately, the more we can educate ourselves, our patients and clients, our peers and supervisors, the more we can reduce the harm inherent in any drug use and, for that matter, within any interpersonal therapy.

Find the others. Teach them and learn from them. And enjoy this wonderful book.

—Julie Holland, MD

# Introduction

Psychedelic experiences are often compared to traveling. One starts with an intention (to relax, to explore, to learn, etc.), chooses a method of transportation, makes arrangements for daily responsibilities during one's absence, and embarks. Most travelers will tell you that preparedness is essential. So is flexibility and readiness for the unexpected. After traveling for a time, one returns home—likely with feelings that range from rejuvenated and inspired to grateful for a good night's rest in one's own bed.

These days there's a lot of media coverage about psychedelics. You can learn about them from popular magazines, prime-time news, late night TV, *New York Times* bestselling books, even a Netflix series. But reliable and practical information for those who use psychedelics can be hard to come by, and most sources don't go into enough depth to give people something they can really use. In this book, we guide you through the process of preparing for a psychedelic experience, taking a psychedelic, and returning from the journey.

Psychedelics have shown potential to be beneficial for spiritual growth, mental health, and general wellness. That said, in this book we also look at methods to reduce potential harm and enhance the potential for benefit from a psychedelic experience. We do this with the intention of facilitating your decision process so you can take the reins and determine—at every juncture—the best course of action for you.

Based on recent research conducted by the National Institutes of Health, around 8 percent of American adults aged 19–30 have used a psychedelic in the past year (Patrick et al. 2023). This book is for anyone who is interested in using psychedelics, even those who aren't sure whether to go ahead. That includes people who have used psychedelics, are looking for guidance on integrating those experiences into their lives or may be planning for future experiences. This book is also for therapists whose clients are curious about or have used psychedelics and want to take a responsible and respectful approach to these conversations in the clinical setting.

# About the Authors

We are two psychologists who began working together in 2016 after meeting at a psychedelic film screening and recognizing our mutual interest in the field. We both have backgrounds in drug policy and the therapeutic potential of psychedelics and have been involved in the largest and most influential clinical research trials in **psychedelic therapy** of the modern era. Elizabeth started her work on a clinical trial of **psilocybin** for alcohol use disorder after years of studying **addiction** psychology and finding that even the best existing treatments fell far short of what was needed to truly help people. Ingmar discovered the field of psychedelic research when early and small studies of **3,4-methylenedioxymethamphetamine** (MDMA) were beginning to show evidence for therapeutic use. He was instrumental in designing and developing methods for quantifying and improving the role of the therapists in these unique treatments.

Our work over the past five years has focused on building Fluence, a platform to provide education and training for clinicians working in psychedelic therapy. Together with our team, we've trained thousands of therapists working in community practice settings, and hundreds more working on clinical research trials of psychedelic therapies. We've also trained practitioners for work with psilocybin in Oregon and Colorado—states in which this is allowed under the local legal frameworks.

In 2021 we published the seminal research paper "Psychedelic Harm Reduction and Integration: A Transtheoretical Model for Clinical Practice" (Gorman et al. 2021), which defines the Psychedelic Harm Reduction and Integration (PHRI) model we elaborate on in this book. PHRI is the foundational model for all of our programs at Fluence, and this book extends and builds on all that we've learned from our fellow trainers and students. We continue to be involved in the leading psychedelic therapy research trials, policy discussions, and key decisions that are shaping the future of the field. Although the past decade has been one of immense growth of the field, we anticipate further expansion as interest in psychedelics becomes more widely accepted and barriers to access are removed.

# The PHRI Model

PHRI draws on current research, finding ways to let research inform the best choices for taking psychedelics in other settings. It incorporates key themes of harm reduction psychotherapy (Tatarsky 2007), psychedelic therapy research, relational psychodynamic therapy, and mindfulness-based therapies. Relational psychodynamic approaches help us understand the importance of the interpersonal context in which psychedelics are used. Mindfulness-based therapies enable us to draw from a rich literature of methods for working with introspective experiences in the service of positive change. Psychedelic therapy research provides the best and most current practices regarding preparation, in-session precautions and procedures, integration, and aftercare in the event of distress. We also discuss the most current ethical standards in the field so readers will be armed with the best information about what is and is not acceptable behavior on the part of providers.

Some of the key themes that we reiterate throughout this book are safety, ethics, intentions, **openness and curiosity**, **embodied integration**, and **values-based action**.

- Safety refers to promoting your (or your client's) physical, psychological, and emotional safety and well-being before, during, and after a psychedelic experience. Safety includes preparation to reduce risk, planning for how to respond to emergencies, and setting boundaries around touch before a psychedelic session.

- Ethics, for psychotherapists, refers to providing psychedelic therapies in ways that are aligned with the principles of your profession, including the unique situations that arise when psychedelic states become part of treatment. From the psychedelic user's perspective, ethics can guide how you choose who you use psychedelics with and how you respond to questions or requests for guidance from your peers.

- Intentions are areas of life in which you hope to progress, grow, or heal though your psychedelic experience. Intentions can act as guideposts for your psychedelic journey.

- Openness and curiosity refer to the willingness to embrace a psychedelic experience as it occurs, allowing it to unfold without judgment or the need for immediate interpretation.

- Embodied integration means taking actions aligned with your experience and insights; in other words, when you make changes in your life based on insights.

- Values-based action is a self-determined, concrete way of engaging with an identified value in a new way; for example, when someone begins volunteering at an animal shelter after realizing just how important animals are to them during their psychedelic session.

PHRI evolved out of what we were seeing in our consultation rooms, while talking with real clients and working with the questions and issues they presented. Some therapists base their approach on knowledge of brain **chemistry** or on abstract research on animals. However, we found that our clients had questions and needs that went beyond the scope of what we could address using such theories. That prompted us to start developing a new approach that fits what we were actually witnessing with our clients, a **practice-based** model.

Harm reduction was once considered a radical departure from models that further stigmatize, exclude, and punish people who engage in any risky behavior. But now it is a respected approach taken by clinicians and public health authorities alike. Still, there are those who preach punishment over treatment. We've seen this pattern time and time again. Either they hold a moralistic view of consequences, or would rather turn a blind eye to the suffering of community members. We conceived of this book as a way to combat the stigma and exclusion faced by so many people who choose to use psychedelics—in any setting and for any reason. If you've ever received a questioning gaze or critical comment when you've discussed your interest in psychedelics, or been afraid to even bring it up with your family, coworkers, teachers, or doctors, this book is here to support you.

"But psychedelics aren't harmful like other drugs," you may say. It is true: psychedelics have a very different risk profile from alcohol, **opiates**, and other drugs that people become addicted to. Most psychedelics don't cause physiological dependence (**tolerance** and **withdrawal**), nor do they typically lead to a pattern of compulsive use. People use them for different reasons, many of which have to do with self-growth, healing from illness, connecting with others, and spirituality. The potential harms that come with psychedelics are largely psychological in nature. They can include lasting disorientation, emotional struggles, and spiritual crises. Occasionally, we see intense emotional distress, **paranoia**, or a feeling of being separate from one's surroundings (**derealization**). For those who already have a mental health condition, the use of psychedelics may increase the risk of suicide or loss of touch with reality. Yet while no guarantee of absolute safety can be made, there are a number of things that can be done to reduce these risks or mitigate negative outcomes should they occur.

Specific adaptations of harm reduction approaches for psychedelic users have a long history of peer efforts at festivals like Burning Man and Boom, as well as through websites and user forums. At festival events, groups of trained volunteers set up sites to receive and care for people who have taken psychedelics and need assistance during the acute phase of their experiences. Such organizations also provide—to varying degrees—education, drug testing services for harmful **adulterants**, and assistance with connecting to community services. Like other harm reduction service providers, these groups have been accused of promoting drug use; some have even been banned through laws that prohibit offering a space in which drug use can take place. While this book does not serve to replace such services, it can help users of psychedelics educate themselves about how and when to access them. This book also expands on peer-based harm reduction efforts with advice and details based on the latest research into the use of psychedelics in therapy.

# Similarities and Differences between PHRI and Psychedelic-Assisted Psychotherapy

If you are seeking the assistance of a professional, it is important to know what type of services they provide. **Psychedelic-assisted psychotherapy** (PAP) includes the administration of a psychedelic in the context of clinical treatment, along with preparation and integration work. We prefer to call it simply psychedelic therapy, as we find that the words *assisted* and *psychotherapy* put the emphasis on psychotherapy that is being enhanced or improved by the addition of a psychedelic session. Psychedelic therapy, to our minds, includes approaches that rely on the **pharmacologic** effects of the psychedelic, whether or not a trained counselor is present. You will see both terms used in this book.

PHRI doesn't include the administration of a psychedelic. However, it can be helpful when someone is taking a psychedelic outside of the clinical setting.

Here are some key similarities and differences between the two approaches.

PAP and PHRI are similar in that they both:

- Recognize the potential benefits of psychedelic experiences for personal growth, healing, or alleviating suffering.

- Involve thorough screening/assessment procedures to determine appropriateness.

- Emphasize preparation and integration of the psychedelic experience.

- Aim to provide a safe container and support for psychedelic experiences.

- Take a nonjudgmental, client-centered approach focused on the individual's inner-directed process.

- Involve developing a strong therapeutic alliance as a foundation.

- Require specialized training for therapists working with psychedelic experiences.

- Emphasize the importance of **set and setting** in shaping psychedelic experiences. Set—short for mindset—is the conscious and unconscious attitudes of the individual person, such as their beliefs, fears, or expectations. Setting is the physical space, environment, and context in which one experiences the effects of the psychedelic drug (for example, music, safety equipment, relationship with session monitors, etc.).

- Take a holistic view, considering biological, psychological, and social factors that influence psychedelic use.

- Encourage a curious, open-minded stance when working with psychedelic states of consciousness.

PAP and PHRI differ in the following ways:

- PAP involves the administration of a psychedelic compound; PHRI does not include providing or administering psychedelics.

- PAP provides psychological support during the actual psychedelic experience; PHRI does not include being present with the client during their psychedelic experience.

- PAP takes place in controlled settings with set protocols; PHRI is intended to help with people using psychedelics in various contexts.

- Often, the goal of PAP is to treat a specific diagnosis; PHRI aims to provide broad support around psychedelic experiences.

- PAP assumes the client's willingness to take psychedelics as a treatment (after proper informed consent processes); PHRI draws on harm reduction principles to meet clients where they are at, even if they are not currently using psychedelics, are unsure about using psychedelics, or changing their psychedelic use patterns.

# How to Use This Book

Readers who are just beginning to learn about psychedelics will benefit from the early chapters, which discuss the context of psychedelics, provide an overview of drug types, and focus on preparation. Those who've already had an experience may want to skip to the later chapters on integration. Experienced users who already know about harm reduction approaches may benefit from reviewing the entire book for new ideas. Each chapter includes exercises for you to help prepare for and personalize your experience. Although these exercises can be done in any order, readers will benefit from completing some exercises before others. At the end of the book, you will find a glossary with definitions of all of the terms you see in bold the first time they appear.

Another important aspect of this book is the reference list. We cite peer-reviewed literature and books throughout the text, and you can find information for every one of our sources in the reference list. If you are especially interested in any particular topic area, we suggest you look it up online and read more. Additionally, you can find worksheet versions of many of this book's exercises at http://www.newharbin ger.com/54254. And you'll find a series of demonstration videos and guided meditations that will comple-ment this book at http://www.fluencetraining.com/PHRI-Therapy-Workbook. If you are a therapist, we encourage you to try out the exercises yourself (actual use of psychedelics is optional!) and choose some to incorporate into your practice. Appendix A consists of a list of resources you can use to find out more about the topics covered in this book. Clinicians will be especially interested in Appendix B, which pro-vides two detailed case examples applying the PHRI model.

# CHAPTER 1

# Psychedelics in Context

In this chapter we look at the origins of psychedelic use and how it has evolved over time. We then focus on the current status of psychedelics, including the regulations and programs relevant to their use.

# Psychedelic Use Through the Ages

The history of psychedelic use has created a rich, intricate tapestry that deeply influences contemporary perceptions and experiences.

## The Early Days

This journey begins with **indigenous** practices. Psychedelics, such as psilocybin mushrooms, **peyote**, and **ayahuasca**, have been used in spiritual and healing ceremonies for hundreds (Samorini 2019) and in some cases, thousands of years (Carod-Artal 2015). In these traditions, psychedelics are not merely tools for altering consciousness but are revered as sacred, enabling profound connections to the spiritual world and providing healing. The belief systems and rituals in these communities ensured that psychedelic use was fundamentally connected to spirituality, healing, and community.

Beginning in the late 1800s and continuing through the mid-twentieth century, researchers in the United States, Canada, and Europe became interested in psychedelic compounds and began to explore their potential within Western medical practices (Gouzoulis-Mayfrank et al. 1998). Research projects included anthropological studies on naturalistic use, basic **chemistry**, and **pharmacology**. They also included treatment studies on the use of psychedelic compounds for people with mental health and addiction problems. Although **synthesized** forms of **mescaline** and psilocybin were already available, **lysergic acid diethylamide** (LSD; commonly called acid), first synthesized in 1938 (Lee and Shlain 1992), was most widely used in human research and treatment during the 1950s and '60s.

By the 1960s, an era of vibrant sociopolitical activism, psychedelics were becoming tools for exploring consciousness and expanding the mind beyond the perceived limitations imposed by prevailing society. This attitude led to widespread recreational use of psychedelics outside of medical or research settings, often divorced from the rituals and safeguarded practices of indigenous cultures. Psychedelics became symbols of the counterculture and rebellion, leading to legal clampdowns and stigma attached to their use.

Beginning in 1953, the U.S. Central Intelligence Agency conducted psychedelic research through Project MK-Ultra, a covert program researching mind control and chemical interrogation methods (Lee and Shlain 1992). This research involved numerous experiments using LSD and other drugs. The program conducted over 150 experiments on humans in universities, hospitals, and prisons in the United States and

Canada, often without the full knowledge or consent of the participants. The program was halted in 1973 and became public knowledge in 1975. It is unknown how many participants were involved in the experiments.

## The Age of Stigma

The period extending from the mid-1970s through the mid-1990s marked a stark hiatus in psychedelic research. Psychedelic use in 1960s counterculture had come to symbolize rebellion, a defiance of establishment norms, and an embrace of alternative lifestyles, all of which were often perceived as threats to society. The association with antiestablishment movements and unconventional ideologies thus made psychedelics a target for political and social denunciation, leading to stringent prohibitions on their use.

There are other reasons why research on the use of psychedelic drugs in psychiatry was abandoned. Following the **thalidomide disaster** in 1963, tighter regulations were imposed on pharmaceutical research. These laws caught psychedelic drugs in their net. As well, the special challenges presented by psychedelics in randomized, placebo-controlled trials during the 1970s made it difficult to reproduce the promising claims made in the 1950s and 1960s. Clinical research became even more difficult after 1965, when the pharmaceutical company Sandoz ceased providing psychedelics for research, and nonmedical use was officially prohibited in 1970 (Hall 2022).

These obstacles drastically hindered scientific explorations into the potential benefits of psychedelics. Psychedelics such as LSD, psilocybin, and mescaline were classified as **Schedule 1** drugs because of their high potential for abuse and no accepted medical use. Researchers faced huge barriers when trying to get funding, approval, and resources for studying these substances that were not just stigmatized but illegal. As a result, academic and scientific researchers did not follow up on the promising results of earlier studies into their therapeutic potential, particularly in mental health contexts.

Research with psilocybin and LSD ground to a halt. An entire generation of scientists and clinicians had no opportunity to research or work directly with psychedelics. The 1980s saw an intensified crackdown on drug use under President Reagan, who initiated the War on Drugs, a program of more stringent policies and aggressive law enforcement against drug possession and distribution. The president's wife, Nancy Reagan, also instituted the Just Say No campaign to discourage drug use. The new narrative, shrouded in fear and moral panic, regarded scientific interest in psychedelics with skepticism and apprehension.

This stigma extended to the discourse on psychedelics. Skepticism, fueled by misinformation and unfounded assumptions, was compounded by dissociation from traditional use of these substances. Even in the mental health profession, psychedelic use was relegated to the fringes instead of being embraced for its potential to facilitate profound healing and transformation. A deep caution became ingrained in generations of medical professionals, scientists, and policymakers.

Consequently, public attitudes toward psychedelic use remained suspended between acknowledging traditional therapeutic use and the association with rebellion, experimentation, and indulgence. The challenge for researchers was to meticulously unravel these layers of stigma and apprehension, providing a balanced, evidence-based, and respectful approach that honors both the potential and the complexities of psychedelics.

This was not an easy task. The stigma surrounding psychedelic use was pervasive, hindering open dialogue and exploration in therapeutic contexts. Clinicians may have feared that expressing interest in research on or therapeutic use of psychedelics could potentially tarnish their professional credibility or alienate them from more conservative or cautious peers or institutions. Such fears inhibited their capacity to explore, understand, and integrate psychedelic therapies into their practice. Users feared judgment, social isolation, and legal issues, dissuading them from sharing their experiences or seeking guidance from healthcare professionals. Thus, stigma obscured pathways for safe, supported, and informed psychedelic use, forcing clinicians and users to navigate psychedelic use with trepidation. The silence and misapprehension veiling psychedelic use stifled the evolution of a comprehensive, empathetic, and evidence-based understanding of psychedelics.

## The Return of Clinical Research

Recent research into the therapeutic applications of psychedelics, particularly in mental health, reflects an emerging synthesis of historical wisdom and modern science. In the early 1980s, anticipating a government ban on the then-unscheduled MDMA (commonly known as Ecstasy), Rick Doblin started the Multidisciplinary Association for Psychedelic Studies (MAPS) (Passie 2023). This fledgling nonprofit supported advocacy efforts at the federal level to keep MDMA available for medical use. When the U.S. Drug Enforcement Agency (DEA) decided to place MDMA on Schedule 1 in 1985, the association moved to support clinical research studies of MDMA that could qualify for U.S. Food and Drug Administration (FDA) approval (Riedlinger 1985).

In the 1990s, research into psychedelics entered a new era (Strassman 1995), particularly within the realm of psychiatric research. In the early 2000s, a modest number of researchers began expressing interest in the psychological and therapeutic potentials of substances like LSD, psilocybin, and MDMA. Research findings on the medical potential of psilocybin (Moreno et al. 2006) and MDMA (Bouso et al. 2008) began to be published.

As the calendar flipped into the 2010s, more trials studying psychedelics began to be published. This research showed that psychedelics could help with depression (Carhart-Harris et al. 2016), anxiety (Ross et al. 2016), **post-traumatic stress disorder** (PTSD) (Mithoefer et al. 2013), and addiction (Garcia-Romeu, Griffiths, and Johnson 2014)—sometimes more effectively than conventional treatment. These results inspired further exploration. Researchers came up with better methods that were more closely aligned with the expectations and standards of the scientific community—meaning their results could stand up to critical review by others. Meanwhile, organizations and institutes dedicated to such research learned how to navigate regulatory mazes.

The following exercise asks you to reflect on the history of psychedelic research.

## Reflecting on Ethical Perspectives in Psychedelic Use

What was your reaction to learning about experiments conducted on LSD use without the participants' consent?

_____

_____

_____

How much information do you think should be available to people who are considering using psychedelics?

_____

_____

_____

Do you personally feel that there is still a stigma associated with the use of psychedelics?

_____

_____

_____

How do you think the traditional use of psychedelics in indigenous cultures differs from the way they are used in modern therapeutic settings? What can contemporary practices learn from these traditions?

_____

_____

_____

_____

Reflecting on the history of government-sanctioned experiments such as Project MK-Ultra, how do you think these events have influenced public perception and policies around psychedelics?

_____

_____

_____

_____

Given the resurgence of psychedelic research in recent years, do you think the stigma around their use will diminish over time? Why or why not?

_____

_____

_____

_____

_____

_____

# Cultural Appreciation or Cultural Appropriation?

Cross-cultural exchange of psychedelic practices encompasses a wide spectrum of interactions between indigenous practices and interested outsiders. For example, with tourists venturing to South America to engage in ayahuasca ceremonies, we can observe an intriguing blend of traditional indigenous rituals and adaptations catering to non-indigenous participants. Sometimes these blends seem entirely sparked by outsiders, while other times they are the result of indigenous community members exercising their right to integrate and adapt their practices voluntarily, for their own benefit and the benefit of their communities. While such interactions enable the preservation and global dissemination of indigenous practices, they have also sparked debate. It's crucial to navigate these exchanges with utmost respect toward and acknowledgment of the originating cultures, their sacred practices, history, and present-day needs. Such a respectful attitude will help guard against the rich tapestry of traditional wisdom being diluted or commercialized in a way that strays from its foundational ethos.

Simultaneously, in the Americas and beyond, we are witnessing a fusion wherein indigenous psychedelic practices are being adapted to different cultural and social contexts (Tupper and Labate 2014). In other words, traditional rituals are being reshaped to resonate with contemporary, nonindigenous settings. One example is the burgeoning popularity of **neoshamanic** practices, in which elements of indigenous psychedelic rituals are blended with modern psychotherapeutic techniques to foster healing and spiritual exploration (Gearin 2016).

While this intercultural dialogue has the potential to enrich our collective understanding and use of psychedelic practices, it also invites critical reflection upon the ethics, authenticity, and integrity of such adaptations. It is vital to ensure that these fusions honor the depth, sanctity, and complexities of the original practices while aligning them with the ethical, social, and legal frameworks of new cultural contexts. Thus, adapting psychedelic practices to contemporary contexts requires an intricate interweaving of traditional wisdom, cross-cultural exchanges, and ethical considerations.

**Cultural appropriation** and **cultural appreciation** are two terms often used in discussions about the interaction with and adoption of elements from a culture different from one's own. Though they might seem related, they carry significantly different implications.

- **Cultural appropriation** typically involves borrowing, taking, or utilizing elements of one culture by members of another culture without understanding, respect, or proper acknowledgment of the history, significance, and values behind those elements. This disrespectful approach can make cultural practices, symbols, and artifacts seem trivial or quaint, stripping them of their original meaning and context and leading to misrepresentation and stereotypes.

When an individual from a different cultural background adopts indigenous psychedelic practices as a trendy experience or commodity, devoid of respect or understanding toward their sacredness and traditional significance, it is appropriation. This is especially true if the practices are used in a way that distorts their original cultural context while the outsider profits.

- On the other hand, **cultural appreciation** seeks to understand and learn about another culture with respect and humility, aiming to broaden one's perspective without taking ownership of the practices, symbols, or elements of the explored culture. It emphasizes honoring and giving due credit to the source culture, thereby respecting its history, practices, and meanings.

In the context of psychedelic practices, cultural appreciation might involve individuals educating themselves about indigenous practices, understanding their deep cultural roots, and engaging in them with respect, ideally under the guidance of a knowledgeable practitioner from the indigenous community. Here, there's a conscious effort to respect the traditions without diminishing their original cultural and spiritual significance, and without exploiting them for personal or commercial gain.

In summary, while cultural appropriation and appreciation both involve interaction with elements from different cultures, the key difference lies in the approach, intention, understanding, and respect toward the original culture. The next exercise invites you to reflect on this complicated topic.

# Journaling Assignment

Take at least five minutes to write about times you have observed cultural appropriation and cultural appreciation in your professional or personal life. Reflect on how you were able to differentiate between them.

Consider responding to these writing prompts:

- What are your feelings regarding the cultural appropriation of drug-related rituals? Is this something you worry about?

- How do you think the traditional use of psychedelics in indigenous cultures differs from the way they are used in modern therapeutic settings?

- What can contemporary practices learn from these traditions?

# The Current Situation

Today, robust clinical trials continue to demonstrate the remarkable potential of psychedelics to facilitate mental healing and transformation. The FDA has even bestowed the coveted designation of **breakthrough therapy** on certain forms of psychedelic therapy, such as psilocybin therapy for treatment-resistant depression (Dunn, Freeman, and Dochniak 2019) and MDMA for PTSD (Feduccia et al. 2019). This designation increases the potential for the rescheduling of certain psychedelics if clinical trial data continue to show promise—meaning that they could become available by prescription just like other medications.

Ongoing debates surround the ethical, medical, and cultural implications of psychedelic use. Advocates, policymakers, and researchers grapple with framing guidelines that integrate psychedelics into therapeutic settings while considering potential risks and cultural contexts (McGuire et al. 2024). The journey toward establishing psychedelics as legitimate therapeutic tools continues.

Studies of professionals demonstrate that interest in and optimism for the therapeutic use of psychedelics is increasing (Barnett et al. 2024), yet for most doctors, these drugs remain illegal to prescribe. This duality challenges us to navigate the intricate path of integrating psychedelics responsibly into culture and health practices, respecting their historical significance, and understanding their social implications.

The resurgence of interest in and accompanying excitement over psychedelic medicine involves both potential and risk. The hope of novel, transformative approaches to psychological ailments has as its shadow side the perils of overzealousness. Clinical **effectiveness** still needs to be demonstrated through meticulous, ethically grounded research. Hyperbolic claims of magic cures and the premature roll-out of treatment programs could undermine the genuine progress being made (Yaden, Potash, and Griffiths 2022). We cannot afford to underplay the very real risks of psychedelic use, such as adverse experiences and contraindications (Evans et al. 2023). The importance of structured, supportive environments for psychedelic sessions cannot be overstated.

As we stand on the brink of what could be a new epoch in psychiatric treatment, our challenge is to navigate the path of cautious, ethical, scientifically rigorous exploration. We are still moving, carefully and with respect, toward comprehending and harnessing the full potential of psychedelic medicine.

## Regulations Regarding Medical and Recreational Cannabis

While federal law continues to classify **cannabis** as a Schedule 1 substance, many states have made it legal for medical or recreational use. Policies related to the prescription, purchase, and use of medical cannabis vary widely between states. Currently, 47 states, the District of Columbia, Guam, Puerto Rico, and the U.S. Virgin Islands allow cannabis for medical use. Some of these states permit its use through comprehensive medical-only programs. Others permit only the use of **cannabidiol** (CBD) or low-**tetrahydrocannabinol** (THC) cannabis for state-defined medical conditions. When we wrote this book, 24 states, the District of Columbia, Guam, and North Mariana Islands permitted cannabis use by adults for nonmedical purposes. In spite all of these allowances for medical and nonmedical purposes, the federal status of cannabis still creates complications for businesses that grow, distribute, and sell cannabis. For instance, such businesses can have trouble getting bank accounts, using basic business management software, or writing off their costs when paying taxes. The patchwork of state legislation also leaves cannabis users vulnerable to legal issues when traveling across state lines.

## Employer Pre-Hire and Random Drug Testing

Employer drug testing is an area of drug policy that impacts nearly everyone. Many employers require all potential hires to submit to a drug screening as a condition for employment. These screenings test for controlled substances, illegal drugs, and certain prescription drugs. Such screenings are required by federal agencies and contractors, and those that comply with the Drug-Free Workplace Act of 1988 are eligible to receive funds. State laws defer to federal law, but states may make their own laws beyond federal law. State laws vary regarding pre-employment drug screening and random testing of employees.

At the time this book was being written, some states permitted drug testing only after providing a copy of their policy (Ohio, Oklahoma) or after making a conditional offer of employment (Maine, Rhode Island). In some states, employers may decline to hire anyone who refuses to take a drug test (for example, Arizona and Florida). Vermont allows no random drug testing of employees unless required by federal law; at the other extreme, in Nebraska employees may be terminated for refusing testing.

The variety of state laws regarding the medical and recreational use of marijuana also impacts employer testing for marijuana. Hawaii has no restrictions on pre-employment testing for marijuana. New Jersey employers may not refuse to hire based on positive results from recreational marijuana use in the employee's private time. Some states may conduct random employee drug tests that accommodate medical marijuana users (Delaware, Maine); others do not accommodate medical marijuana users (Georgia, Kentucky). In Ohio, employers may terminate or discipline an employee who fails a test for marijuana. These variations in law, especially when combined with the complexities of cannabis law, can result in confusion and undue stress for employees. Employers, on the other hand, must keep up with different laws in different states in which they do business, a situation that lends itself to mistakes.

# School-Based Drug Prevention Programs

The purpose of school-based programs is to prevent or decrease the use of certain substances among children, including illegal substances like cocaine) and legal but harmful substances such as alcohol and tobacco. Among these programs, one of the most well-known is Drug Abuse Resistance Education (D.A.R.E.). The D.A.R.E. program sends police officers to visit elementary school classrooms to warn children of the dangers from these substances and how to resist peer pressure that might entice them to indulge. Founded in 1983, D.A.R.E was prominent through the 1980s and 1990s; estimates are that its police officers visited 75 percent of American school districts. Results of research on D.A.R.E.'s outcomes have been mixed, with some studies showing no positive impact on long-term reductions in drug abuse (Rosenbaum and Hanson 1998) and mixed impacts of the program's prosocial behavior training (Pan and Bai 2009).

There are other school-based programs with similar goals of drug abuse prevention. Project ALERT aims to prevent substance abuse in 7th and 8th graders. The program includes unlimited student access to online training/support, eReader lesson plans, online interactive videos, student handouts, and classroom posters. The LifeSkills Training program aims to prevent the use of tobacco, alcohol, and marijuana through helping students to understand and resist influences that may promote such use. The program includes structured small-group activities as well as role-playing scenarios to help students develop these skills. LifeSkills Training provides separate programs for grades 3–6, grades 6–9, and grades 9–12.

These programs are only available in some schools, and research on long-term outcomes is lacking. But they do offer promise for addressing the increasing rates of drug use among young people. Unfortunately, programs that expect the individual to control their own drug use may perpetuate the stigma attached to drug use. Effective programs must include education about the importance of social factors as well. Social factors include lack of access to resources, historical oppression, and **intergenerational trauma**.

The next exercise invites you to reflect on your own experiences with drug policy and programs.

# Your Own Experience

There are many ways you might interact with drug policy, even if you aren't using psychedelics. Use the following questions as writing prompts to journal about how drug policy might pertain to you, your family, your friends, colleagues/classmates, etc.

Have you been drug screened or asked to sign a statement consenting to drug screening for employment?

_____

_____

Have you been asked to show identification for buying cold medicine or allergy medicine?

_____

_____

Were you asked to attend a drug prevention program in school? Or were you taught about drugs by your childhood educators?

_____

_____

Has your doctor discussed medical cannabis with you for any indication?

_____

_____

Is cannabis legal for nonmedical use in your state? Do you face stigma for using it even if it is legal?

_____

_____

_____

_____

What precautions or preparations do you take when traveling with controlled substances that are legally prescribed to you?

_____

_____

_____

_____

Are you aware of the local laws regarding possession of drug testing kits, naloxone, and other harm reduction measures as a concerned citizen?

_____

_____

Do you understand your rights and responsibilities regarding participation in any diversion or rehabilitation program should you have an encounter with law enforcement?

_____

_____

What representatives are advancing drug policy reform in your jurisdiction, and have you given them feedback on their proposals?

_____

_____

Have you been targeted by law enforcement for your drug use, or because you belong to a community that is perceived to have a specific pattern of drug use by law enforcement officers? Is this true for other members of your community, and how has it affected you/your community?

_____

_____

_____

_____

_____

_____

_____

_____

# The Lay of the Land: When, Where, and Why Psychedelics?

The decision to use psychedelics is uniquely personal, yet embedded in a web of historical and social context. In this chapter, we explore how you could be affected by the cultural context and meaning of taking a psychedelic and ask you to investigate your own motives.

Motives can range from curiosity or a desire to socialize with others, to deeply held spiritual beliefs (Basedow and Kuitunen-Paul 2022; Pestana, Beccaria, and Petrilli 2021). Your motives might include improving mental health, healing from trauma, or enhancing creativity. There is no wrong reason to use a psychedelic. Understanding your own motivations can help you make sense of your choices and your experience and may help determine which psychedelic you use and in what context.

Consider, for example, how you first heard about psychedelics. Maybe it was from your friends, or during school educational programs about drugs of abuse. Maybe you heard psychedelics mentioned in your favorite songs, or by family members around the dinner table. Maybe you heard of their use in your spiritual tradition, or other traditions that were not familiar to you. You may have experienced curiosity, fear, awe, the desire to try psychedelics, total disinterest, or anything in between. In this chapter, we'll go through a series of exercises to help you reflect on motivations and desires surrounding psychedelic use.

The first exercise is called "Why am I here?" In this context, "here" refers to this juncture in your life, reading this book, having this conversation with yourself (or your therapist or others in your life). "Why am I here?" is a simplified way of asking "What brings me to this decision? What is it that I am truly seeking? What other driving factors are at play?" Take some time to gather this workbook or a journal and a pen, and spend about 10 minutes on this exercise.

# "Why Am I Here?"

**Objective:** This exercise aims to help individuals explore and reflect on their life purpose, goals, and motivations, inspired by the phrase "Why am I here?"

**Instructions:**

1. Consider the phrase "Why am I here?"

2. Write down one thought, feeling, or insight that comes to mind.

   _____

   _____

3. Reflect on the phrase "Why am I here?" again. Write down one thought, feeling, or insight that comes to mind.

   _____

   _____

4. Reflect on the phrase "Why am I here?" once more. Write down one thought, feeling, or insight that comes to mind.

   _____

   _____

5. After reflecting on your three responses, ask yourself, "Is there a common thread or theme?"

6. Write a brief summary of your thoughts and insights from this exercise. Consider how you can use this newfound understanding moving forward.

   _____

   _____

Remember, this exercise is for your personal reflection and growth. It is important to be honest with yourself. The insights you gain can help guide you toward your upcoming experience.

The next exercise explores how your individual identity—your sense of self, belief systems, and values—may be affected by a psychedelic experience. Research has demonstrated that people can experience profound shifts in their sense of self (Letheby and Gerrans 2017), a realignment with their values (Kähönen 2023), and even a new understanding of the nature of reality through the use of psychedelics (Miller 2024). While such outcomes have been best documented in supported settings, they are known to occur when people take psychedelics on their own or with peer groups, without any intent to have a life-transforming outcome. This exercise will help you explore what you consider to be the most fundamental aspects of your very nature, what you take for truth and hold most valuable as you prepare for potential shifts or deepening of your awareness.

# Reflecting on Values and Beliefs

**Objective:** This exercise aims to help individuals explore and identify aspects of their lives, beliefs, and values they feel unequivocally sure about, promoting self-awareness and also possibility for change.

**Instructions:** Reflect on each of the categories. Under each heading, write down any thoughts, beliefs, or experiences you feel absolutely certain about.

*Personal beliefs:* Consider your core beliefs about yourself, others, and the world around you. What are the beliefs that you hold with unwavering conviction?

_____

_____

*Values:* Reflect on your values, the guiding principles that shape your decisions and actions. What values do you feel deeply committed to and sure about?

_____

_____

*Life experiences:* Think about significant life events or experiences that have shaped who you are today. What lessons or insights have you gained from these experiences that you feel certain about?

_____

_____

Once you have completed your list, take a moment to review your responses. Reflect on the following questions:

- How do your values and beliefs influence your actions and decisions in daily life?

- Do you have any doubts about the items in this list? What are they?

_____

_____

_____

_____

_____

_____

_____

You may wish to look back at this list during the integration phase.

The next exercise is geared toward your specific motives for seeking a psychedelic experience—whether or not you've already had one. Remember, motives can be different for every person, and they can be different at different times. Some people sense their motivation changing as they get more experience with psychedelics, which seems natural.

It may also be helpful to distinguish between intrinsic and extrinsic motivation. Intrinsic means it comes from within you, such as a desire to feel something pleasurable. Extrinsic means it comes from outside you, like following the recommendation of a therapist or friend. In many cases, both may be present.

## Identifying Your Motives for Using Psychedelics

**Objective:** This exercise aims to help you explore and understand your motivations for using psychedelics, considering potential benefits, risks, and personal values.

**Instructions:** Reflect on each of the categories, and under each heading, write down any reasons, feelings, or thoughts that you have related to using psychedelics in that context. Take your time and be honest with yourself. The following questions may help:

*Curiosity and exploration:* Are you drawn to psychedelics because you're curious about the experience or the potential insights they might provide? Are you seeking a new perspective on life or a deeper understanding of yourself?

_____

_____

_____

*Personal growth:* Do you believe that psychedelics can help you grow personally, spiritually, or emotionally? Are there specific aspects of your life or character that you hope to improve or transform through the use of psychedelics?

_____

_____

_____

*Therapeutic benefits:* Are you considering using psychedelics to address mental health issues, emotional trauma, or addiction? Have you researched the potential therapeutic benefits and risks associated with psychedelic use?

_____

_____

_____

*Social connections:* Are you drawn to psychedelics because of the social aspect or to connect with a specific community? Do you hope to bond with others through shared psychedelic experiences?

_____

_____

_____

*Recreation:* Are you interested in using psychedelics for fun or enjoyment? Do you view them as a way to get away from daily life or to experience a different way of being?

_____

_____

_____

Once you have completed your list, take a moment to review your responses. Reflect on the following questions:

• Are your motivations aligned with your personal values?

• Are there any potential risks or negative consequences associated with your motivations?

• How might you ensure that your psychedelic use is responsible and beneficial to your well-being?

Write a brief summary of your thoughts and insights from this exercise, considering how you can use this newfound understanding of your motivations to make informed decisions about your psychedelic use.

_____

_____

_____

_____

_____

_____

Remember, this exercise is for your personal reflection and growth. It is important to be honest with yourself and consider the potential benefits, risks, and implications of your motivations.

We have explored the broader context of your interest in psychedelics as well as your personal motivations for taking a psychedelic. Now let's focus on individual factors that can influence your experience. We use the term **biopsychosocial** to mean the connected biological, psychological, and social factors that each individual experiences (George and Engel 1980). Here, things can get specific according to the psychedelic you are considering. For example, if you are thinking of taking a psychedelic for your mental health, but you are also taking a medication for psychological symptoms, it's possible that medication could interact with that psychedelic. This would be a biological factor that also relates to psychological risk. Remember, coming off of a medication can be psychologically challenging and may lead to a recurrence of the symptoms for which you took the medication in the first place. Ultimately the decision about what to do is up to you and your doctor. There is no single right answer for everyone.

In this next exercise, the idea is simply to list out all the factors you can think of so you can reflect on them. Sometimes, just putting them down on paper makes it easier to see how they relate to each other and helps you to make a decision that is right for you.

## Identifying Your Biopsychosocial Factors Influencing Psychedelic Experiences

**Objective:** This exercise aims to help you explore and understand the various factors that could influence a psychedelic experience, including your personal history, biology, psychology, and social context. If you feel you don't know much about some of these areas, make note of them. We'll be covering all of these areas in more detail later in this book.

**Instructions:** Reflect on each of the categories. Under each heading, write down any relevant factors, experiences, or personal traits that you believe could influence your psychedelic experience.

*Biological Factors:* Consider aspects of your physical health, genetics, and any medical conditions that might affect your psychedelic experience. Some examples include your age, sex, illnesses, neurodivergence, and any medications you are taking.

_____

_____

_____

_____

_____

*Psychological Factors:* Reflect on your mental health, emotional well-being, and personality traits. Consider any history of mental health disorders, past traumas, or significant life events that could influence your experience with psychedelics.

_____

_____

_____

_____

_____

_____

*Social Factors:* Think about your cultural background, social support network, and relationships with others. Consider how these factors could impact your set and setting during a psychedelic experience, as well as your ability to integrate the experience afterward.

_____

_____

_____

_____

_____

_____

Once you have completed your list, take a moment to review your responses. Reflect on the following questions:

- Are there any factors that could potentially increase the risks or challenges associated with your psychedelic experience? How might you address or avoid these concerns?

- Are there any factors that could contribute positively to your psychedelic experience? How can you enhance or emphasize these aspects during your experience?

- How can you use this understanding of your biopsychosocial factors to better prepare for and navigate a psychedelic experience?

_____

_____

_____

_____

_____

_____

_____

Again, this exercise is for your personal reflection and growth. There is no single right answer that applies to everyone. The goal is to find clarity by listing out the factors that influence your decision.

Now, consider the setting in which you choose to take a psychedelic (Golden et al. 2022). We can assure you that people have taken psychedelics (or found themselves on one) in nearly every setting imaginable. Some settings seem to be much more conducive to safe experience than others, and some are outright inadvisable (for example, while driving!). Some settings may be more manageable for experienced psychedelic users than for those who are just starting out. We encourage you to plan accordingly. Always err on the side of caution.

Complete the following exercise to explore the factors in the setting you are considering.

# Factors that Influence a Setting for a Psychedelic Experience

**Objective:** Environmental factors play a significant role in shaping a psychedelic experience. This exercise identifies some common and important environmental factors when choosing a setting for psychedelic use. It gives you the opportunity to analyze your choice of setting and decide which factors to change ahead of your experience.

- *Safety:* A familiar, safe, and comfortable environment, such as one's home or a close friend's house, can promote a sense of security and ease during the experience.

- *Cleanliness:* A clean and uncluttered space can reduce distractions and create more peace of mind.

- *Lighting:* Soft, natural, or dimmed lighting creates a more relaxing and soothing ambiance.

- *Temperature:* A comfortable room temperature and providing options for warmth or cooling (blankets, fans) can help manage one's comfort during the experience.

- *Sound:* A quiet environment with minimal background noise or disturbances can promote introspection. If desired, ambient sounds, nature sounds, or music can be used to create a supportive soundscape.

- *Comfortable seating and resting areas:* Comfortable seating options, such as cushions, bean bags, or a soft couch, can help accommodate various postures during the experience.

- *Personalized decorations and objects:* Meaningful artwork, plants, or personal items can create a more personalized supportive environment.

- *Access to outdoor spaces:* If possible, access to a safe and peaceful outdoor area, such as a garden or patio, can provide opportunities for connecting with nature during the experience.

- *Privacy:* A sufficient level of privacy can contribute to feelings of ease and reduce the potential for unwanted interruptions or disturbances.

- *Proximity to necessities:* Easy access to restrooms, water, and food.

- *Disconnection from technology:* Electronic devices can be turned off or left in another room to minimize distractions. Note: Have a phone accessible in case of an urgent need.

In the table below, write down the setting you are thinking of taking a psychedelic in, and then a few words of reflection on how well it matches each of the points above, following the example below:

| | | Alternate setting A: | Alternate setting B: |
|---|---|---|---|
| **Location:** | My bedroom | | |
| **Safety:** | Yes, very safe | | |
| **Cleanliness** | A bit cluttered… | | |
| **Lighting** | Perfect lighting | | |
| **Temperature** | I can control it | | |
| **Sound** | I can use my own stereo and a playlist for music | | |
| **Comfortable seating** | Very good | | |
| **Personalized** | Maybe too many difficult memories? | | |
| **Outdoor access** | Only if I go downstairs to the yard | | |
| **Privacy** | Yes, if I don't go downstairs to the yard | | |
| **Proximity** | Yes | | |
| **Disconnection** | Yes | | |

Now that you've reflected on the setting or settings you are considering, write about any changes you would like to make to help yourself have an experience that is more aligned with your motivations for the psychedelic experience. What recurring themes or key phrases do you see in your responses to the prompts across all of these exercises? What new things have you learned about yourself and your motivations by engaging with this process? What factors or considerations are influencing your decision that you weren't aware of before?

_____

_____

_____

_____

_____

_____

_____

The final exercise in this chapter will help you decide whether to proceed with your chosen plan. You may decide to go back to the drawing board, give it some more time, or find an alternative path toward your true goals. Remember, the decision is yours to make; the knowledge you've gained here will help.

> **Hint:** If you are preparing for an experience that will be provided by a psychedelic therapist or facilitator of any kind, you can ask about these aspects of the setting to better learn what to expect. These factors will be familiar to any provider who is trained in the current best practices for psychedelic therapy or facilitation, and also apply to spiritual settings.

## Creating a Pros and Cons List for a Psychedelic Experience

**Objective:** This exercise aims to help you evaluate your personal reasons for considering a psychedelic experience. Creating a list of pros and cons can assist you in making an informed decision.

**Instructions:** Take a moment to consider your motivations, expectations, and concerns related to a psychedelic experience. Think about the potential benefits and risks, as well as your personal readiness and circumstances.

In the "Pros" column, list any positive aspects or potential benefits you associate with a psychedelic experience. Some factors to consider might include:

- Personal growth and self-discovery

- Enhanced creativity and problem-solving

- Emotional healing or processing of past traumas

- Deepening spiritual connection or exploration

- Strengthening relationships and empathy

In the "Cons" column, list any potential risks, concerns, or drawbacks you associate with a psychedelic experience. Some factors to consider might include:

- Possible adverse physical or psychological effects

- Legal or social consequences

- The potential for a challenging or overwhelming experience

- The cost and time commitment involved

| Pros | Cons |
|------|------|
|      |      |

Once you have completed both columns, take a moment to review your list. Reflect on the following questions:

- How do the pros and cons weigh against each other? Do the potential benefits outweigh the risks, or vice versa?

- Are there any concerns or risks that you can address or avoid through careful planning and preparation?

- Are you currently in the right place, mentally and emotionally, to have a psychedelic experience? If not, what changes could you make to better prepare yourself?

_____

_____

_____

_____

_____

_____

_____

The next chapters take us into the details of selecting a psychedelic, choosing a setting, and making final preparations. Even if you aren't sure that you are ready to take a psychedelic or are thinking it is best to hold off for the time being, these chapters may still be useful.

# CHAPTER 3

# Nuts and Bolts

Now that you have some background about psychedelics and have reflected on your own beliefs and attitudes toward them, we will turn to some concrete information you'll need so you can make informed decisions. There is a lot to learn about psychedelics; a simple internet search can turn up an overwhelming number of sources. Some of the hardest choices may be just figuring out which sources to trust and how to sift through the information!

Fortunately, we have been immersed in this topic for years. We have distilled some of the most important points for you, and we provide you with a list of sources in Appendix A that you can use to find out more, if you wish. Remember, there's a glossary of terms at the back of the book that will help you as well.

This chapter provides information about the various kinds of psychedelic substances, their typical effects, and dose ranges. These data are based on empirical studies conducted in controlled settings. We also share the current understanding of psychiatric and medical contraindications. It is important to note that these risks are still not fully understood and are part of ongoing research. Additionally, if you are a therapist, it is essential that you do not provide medical advice to your clients if you are not licensed to do so. The purpose of providing this information is to educate the reader, not as guidelines for recommendations or prescription by clinicians. This information is not a substitute for individualized medical advice.

# Drug Classifications

Psychedelics can be classified by their chemical structure and mechanism of action. All of them produce changes in perception, mood, and cognitive processes. They vary in their precise subjective effects and the ways they work in the human brain. Psychedelics are categorized into chemical families, notably **tryptamines**, **phenethylamines**, and **ergolines**.

Tryptamines are **serotonergic hallucinogens** (Araújo et al. 2015). They include psilocybin, found in certain species of mushrooms. These compounds can produce significant alterations in sensory perception, thought, and mood in humans.

Phenethylamines are a class of chemicals found in certain plants and animals (Nichols 1981). This group includes mescaline, which is present in the peyote cactus. Mescaline is known for its mood and perception-altering effects.

Ergolines, such as LSD, are **semisynthetic** compounds derived from lysergic acid, which occurs naturally in specific fungi like ergot and in some species of morning glory seeds. While ergolines like LSD are recognized for their potent hallucinogenic effects, others, such as ergotamine, are used for medical purposes and do not have hallucinogenic properties (Mantegani, Brambilla, and Varasi 1999).

In practice, psychedelics have overlapping subjective effects and can be categorized broadly into four common types of drugs:

1. **Classic Psychedelics:** These drugs are found in or are derived from plants that have a long history of use in many indigenous cultures. They produce visual and sometimes auditory hallucinations (Muttoni, Ardissino, and John 2019). This group includes:

   o *LSD:* A potent semisynthetic psychedelic known to induce psychedelic effects even at tiny doses and lasting up to 12 hours. Less intense but still noticeable effects can linger up to 24 hours.

   o *Psilocybin:* Found in "magic mushrooms" or synthesized. Commonly used in psychedelic research. Is known for inducing psychedelic states lasting around 4–6 hours.

   o *DMT (***dimethyltryptamine***):* A powerful but short-acting psychedelic found in several plants. Can be synthesized.

   o *Mescaline:* Derived from the peyote and San Pedro cacti; often synthesized; known for its intense psychoactive effects.

2. **Dissociative Psychedelics:** These drugs are known as dissociative because they distort perception of sight and sound and can cause feelings of detachment from their environment and from one's self (Denomme and Heifets 2024). This group includes:

   o *Ketamine:* Initially developed as an **anesthetic.** Can induce dissociative states and acute psychedelic effects.

   o *PCP* (**phencyclidine**): Known for its dissociative effects; can also cause psychedelic effects, **delirium**, and **mania**.

   o *DXM* (dextromethorphan): Commonly found in cough syrups. At high doses it can produce effects similar to classic psychedelics.

3. **Empathogens or Entactogens:** These drugs cause an individual to experience feelings of emotional communion, oneness, relatedness, and empathy or sympathy (Nichols 2022). This group includes:

   o *MDMA:* Known commonly as Ecstasy or Molly. It enhances feelings of empathy and emotional closeness.

   o *MDEA (***methyldiethanolamine***):* Has effects similar to MDMA.

4. **Atypical Psychedelics:** Like other psychedelics, these drugs produce mind-altering effects but have different mechanisms of action. The experience their use induces may be very different from that produced by classic psychedelics. This group includes:

   o *Ayahuasca:* A brew made by Amazonian shamans from plants containing DMT and other psychoactive substances. Results in a powerful experience (see About Ayahuasca below).

   o *Salvia divinorum*: A plant that produces short-lasting but intense hallucinations and altered visual perceptions.

   o *Ibogaine:* Derived from the African *Taburnathe iboga* shrub. Traditionally used by followers of the Bwiti religion in Gabon, Cameroon, and the Republic of Congo. Ibogaine is known for its use in treating addiction and its intense, long-lasting psychedelic effects.

   o *Amanita Muscaria (Fly Agaric) mushrooms:* Several subspecies of mushrooms with varying properties and hallucinogenic effects, traditionally used by indigenous people of Serbia.

There are hundreds of other compounds that fall under the category of psychedelics, and thousands more could be developed by chemists. *PIHKAL*, a classic book by Alexander and Anne Shulgin published in 1990 (Shulgin and Shulgin 1991), documents 179 psychedelic compounds in the phenethylamine category alone.

We provided only these most common categories to give you a basic vocabulary of psychedelic terms. A more in-depth explanation of each psychedelic follows.

# Is Cannabis a Psychedelic?

Cannabis is not considered one of classic psychedelics, though it shares some overlapping effects. The primary psychoactive component of cannabis, THC, can induce alterations in mood, perception, and cognition (Woelfl et al. 2020). However, its **pharmacological profile** and the nature of its psychoactive effects differ significantly from those of classic psychedelics. THC acts on receptors throughout the brain and body that are largely untouched by drugs typically labeled as psychedelics.

The use of cannabis and its derived products like CBD and THC can also result in a pattern of daily use that is not typical of how psychedelics are used. About 10 percent of all cannabis users experience problems with addiction to cannabis (Connor et al. 2021). Although it is a Schedule I drug, cannabis is also widely available in the United States through state programs that regulate its use for both medical and nonmedical purposes.

We know that people often use cannabis together with psychedelics in ceremonial and peer-group settings. Cannabis appears to intensify desired effects or regulate unwanted side effects of psychedelics for some users (Kuc et al. 2022). To date, there hasn't been any clinical research regarding the combined effects for mental health outcomes. In fact, most studies of psychedelics for mental health exclude people who use cannabis because it can be used to treat the same problems, which makes it harder to detect the impact of the psychedelics. This is an area we hope to see more research on in the future!

# Classic Psychedelics

**Pharmacology** is the study of interactions between chemical substances—whether naturally occurring, human-made, or halfway in-between (semisynthetic)—and the brain. Each type of psychedelic has a unique chemical structure and interacts with the brain in different ways. Within each category there are similarities as well as variations, such as intensity and duration of the effects. For example, classic psychedelics share some commonalities in their chemical structures and pharmacology, yet also possess unique characteristics.

A key feature of classic psychedelics is their activity at **serotonin receptors**, especially the 5-HT2A receptor (Cameron et al. 2023). This receptor is widely distributed in the brain and is thought to play a key role in the regulation of mood, thought processing (cognition), and perception. Activation of the 5-HT2A receptor is strongly associated with psychedelic experiences such as changes in sensory perception, thought processes, and emotional states.

For example, one might experience changes in sensory perception by feeling temperature differently or by becoming aware of sensations within the body that are not noticeable. Sight is often enhanced, with people seeing visual illusions like patterns moving or walls appearing to bend and stretch as though they were breathing. The faces of others in the room may look distorted or cartoonish. There are many visual effects that fall short of full hallucinations but can be quite powerful, nonetheless.

Thought processes often shift under the influence of psychedelics (Sayalı and Barrett 2023)—an area of great interest in the world of psychotherapy. This includes experiences like making associations between things that aren't normally seen as connected, having new insights (Tulver et al. 2023), or feeling a deeper sense of understanding the nature of reality.

Sometimes there is a specific thing one wants to consider under the influence of a psychedelic, and in therapy settings it is often the problem one was seeking help with in the first place. Although we don't recommend trying to force yourself to think about a specific topic if it doesn't seem relevant at the time, there is a strong history of people having new insights about what is on their minds. Yet although many individuals do report experiencing helpful insights, it's important to be aware that false insights or beliefs can also arise (McGovern et al. 2024). Psychedelics are not a truth serum.

Shifts in emotional states are also interesting from a psychotherapeutic perspective. Many people naturally feel very good—delighted, happy, content, amused, joyful—during the acute effect phase of classic psychedelics (Goldy et al. 2024). This experience can represent a shift from one's usual state and be a helpful way to experience one's life and relationships for a while. Interestingly, even though these positive moods can be quite powerful, classic psychedelics don't lead to the same patterns of compulsive use that other drugs like alcohol, cocaine, and opiates do (Halberstadt 2015; Bonson 2012). However, one can still become enamored of them and return to them just to experience feeling good.

## LSD

*Chemical structure:* LSD is a semisynthetic compound derived from **ergot alkaloids**, which are produced by a fungus (*Claviceps purpurea*) that grows on rye. Its structure is complex and contains a **bicyclic hexahydroindole ring fused to a bicyclic quinoline group.**

*Pharmacology:* LSD primarily acts as an **agonist** at serotonin receptors, particularly the 5-HT2A receptor. Its effects are thought to be mediated through this interaction. LSD is known for its high potency; even very small doses in micrograms can produce profound effects.

*Effects:* The acute effects of LSD are known to last 10–12 hours. It often induces hallucinations, visions, vivid sensory experiences, ecstatic experiences, heightened awareness or understanding, mixed sensory experiences (seeing sound) and/or spiritual experiences. People who use LSD commonly report intense emotions and drastic changes in **cognition,** including the feeling of increased cognitive clarity, insight, and a profound sense of understanding. Some people have experiences that feel spiritual or have spiritual significance. People sometimes experience muscle tension, jitteriness, and an inability to sleep.

## *PSILOCYBIN*

*Chemical structure:* Psilocybin is a naturally occurring psychedelic compound produced by several species of mushrooms. Chemically, it is an **indolealkylamine**, structurally related to the **neurotransmitter** serotonin.

*Pharmacology:* Psilocybin is a **prodrug**, meaning it is converted in the body to its active form, psilocin. Psilocin acts as an agonist at serotonin receptors, particularly at the 5-HT2A receptor, leading to its psychedelic effects. Psilocybin is **orally active**, and the acute effects usually last around 4–6 hours.

*Effects:* The subjective effects of psilocybin are similar to LSD; however, they tend to be less intense, with a more euphoric mood and fewer unwanted side effects like jitteriness and muscle tension.

Here are a few statements from participants in studies of psilocybin:

"It was like being inside of nature, and I could've just stayed there forever—it was wonderful. All kinds of other things were coming, too, like feelings of being connected to everything, I mean, everything in nature. Everything—even like pebbles, drops of water in the sea … it was like magic. It was wonderful, and it wasn't like talking about it, which makes it an idea, it was, like, experiential. It was like being inside a drop of water, being inside of … a butterfly's wing. And being inside of a cheetah's eyes" (Belser et al. 2017).

"I saw rivers and patterns … I imagined that I could see my capillaries, projecting my skin onto the surface of the scanner, seeing all the corpuscles play to-and-fro."

"I didn't really cognitively think about [the experience], I didn't label what was happening. It was happening, [and] I was preoccupied with it happening."

"Once the drug kicked in, the anxiety changed, and a sense of awe overtook" (Turton, Nutt, and Carhart-Harris 2014).

## DMT

*Chemical structure:* DMT has a simple **tryptamine structure** with two methyl groups attached to the nitrogen atom of the tryptamine backbone. It is structurally similar to serotonin and **melatonin**.

*Pharmacology:* DMT binds to and activates serotonin receptors, mainly the 5-HT2A receptor. It is naturally found in many plants and animals. It can also be synthesized in a lab. DMT isn't orally active unless it is combined with another drug that inhibits its breakdown in the digestive tract—which is what happens when it is included in ayahuasca. Outside of clinical settings, DMT is most often smoked. Clinical researchers are working with injectable or intravenous formulations.

*Effects:* Similar to LSD and psilocybin, but can feel far more intense with a brief but total loss of interaction with the environment. When smoked or injected, DMT's effects can be as short as 15 minutes. When taken orally, the effects may last a few hours.

## MESCALINE

*Chemical structure:* Mescaline is a naturally occurring psychedelic alkaloid of the phenethylamine class, found in certain cacti, including peyote and San Pedro. Its structure is similar to the neurotransmitters **dopamine** and **epinephrine**.

*Pharmacology:* Mescaline works primarily by increasing activity at serotonin receptors, especially the 5-HT2A receptor. It also has an affinity for dopamine receptors, contributing to its psychoactive effects.

*Effects:* The effects of mescaline are described as similar to both LSD and empathogens (see Empathogens below).

## HEALTH RISKS OF CLASSIC PSYCHEDELICS

Classic psychedelics do not typically lead to physical dependence or withdrawal syndromes. They have a low potential for abuse compared to other substances. Tolerance to their effects can develop quickly (de la Fuente Revenga et al. 2022), but it also dissipates quickly after people stop using them. Psilocybin in particular is known for being quite safe in terms of its physiological impacts on the body. However, it does cause a small increase in heart rate and blood pressure during the acute effects (Muttoni, Ardissino, and John 2019), which can be risky for those with untreated hypertension. People can also experience paranoia, delusions, and anxiety during the use of classic psychedelics. These effects are generally fleeting and wear off as the drug dissipates, but some people do experience lingering psychological distress (Evans et al. 2023).

Flashbacks are another potential occurrence after the use of classic psychedelics (Müller et al. 2022). Flashbacks are a reexperiencing of the acute effects long after the drug has dissipated from the body. Sometimes they are tied to stress or other environmental triggers, yet sometimes they seem random. People can experience them as benign or distressing depending on how they may or may not interfere with one's functioning. Hallucinogen Persisting Perceptual Disorder refers to flashbacks after using a psychedelic that cause distress severe enough that the person seeks help (Halpern, Lerner, and Passie 2016).

# Dissociative Psychedelics

Dissociative psychedelics are known for inducing a sense of detachment from reality, including dissociation from oneself and the environment (Paleos 2016). They have unique chemical structures and pharmacological properties and are different in key ways from the classic psychedelics. A defining feature of dissociative psychedelics is their **antagonism** of the N-methyl-D-aspartate **(NMDA) receptor**. This receptor is a major site of action for the primary **excitatory** neurotransmitter in the **central nervous system** (CNS). By blocking these receptors, dissociative psychedelics disrupt normal neural activity. They can produce a sense of detachment or dissociation from the environment and oneself, altered sensory perceptions, and, in some cases, hallucinations.

Recent research, particularly with ketamine, has indicated potential for promoting **neuroplasticity** and rapid antidepressant effects, both of significance to mental health treatment.

## KETAMINE

*Chemical structure:* Ketamine is a synthetic compound, chemically classified as an **arylcyclohexyl-amine**. It structurally resembles PCP and has a *chiral structure*, meaning it exists in two mirror-image forms (enantiomers).

*Pharmacology:* The primary action of ketamine is as an NMDA receptor antagonist. By blocking these receptors, which are a subtype of **glutamate** receptors, ketamine induces its dissociative effects. It also interacts with other receptors, including opioid and **sigma receptors**, contributing to its complex **pharmacological profile**.

*Effects:* Ketamine can cause dreamlike visions and drastically alter mood and behavior.

Here are a few statements from participants in studies of ketamine:

"It's almost like a state of paralysis, where you do receive visual and sound information. But I don't know how much sense I was making to the people in the room around me. It feels like when you try and run in a dream, but your legs won't move fast enough. In fact, exactly like that."

"The experience was genuinely remarkable in terms of both the visual effects and…the sort of removal of ego that accompanied that. I felt that I was one with the whole universe and it sounds hippy dippy but that's how I felt… I think I related to this sort of ego changing, the size of the ego in me as well as a sort of physical sensation."

"…there were pieces that I was familiar with, but they were just, they were coming. It's like different aspects that made up the piece were coming through at different speeds or different pitches. They were just sounding like unique…I could still hear them as piano pieces but they weren't the pieces that I knew" (Mollaahmetoglu et al. 2021).

## PCP

*Chemical structure:* PCP is a synthetic dissociative drug, originally developed as a surgical anesthetic. It is similar in structure to ketamine.

*Pharmacology:* PCP's primary mode of action is as an NMDA receptor antagonist. It also affects other neurotransmitter systems, including dopamine, opioid, and **nicotinic receptors**.

*Effects:* PCP's wide-ranging interaction with various neurotransmitter systems contributes to its potent and sometimes unpredictable effects.

## DXM

*Chemical structure:* DXM is a synthetic compound that binds to sigma opioid receptor sites in the CNS. It has powerful cough suppressant properties.

*Pharmacology:* DXM also acts as an NMDA receptor antagonist. Its **metabolite** dextrorphan binds to phencyclidine receptors, which is thought to be the primary reason for its psychedelic effects ("Dextromethorphan" 2006).

*Effects:* DXM's subjective effects are similar to psilocybin. People report lightheadedness, disembodiment, and nausea, as well as mild mystical-type experiences, insights, and absorption in music (Carbonaro et al. 2018; Reissig et al. 2012).

Dissociative psychedelics can create a profound sense of detachment from the body or environment, often described as an "out-of-body" experience. This can include feeling as if one is floating, observing oneself from a distance, or being disconnected from physical sensations. Auditory distortions are also common, with sounds appearing muffled, amplified, or strangely altered. Visual perceptions might shift, leading to blurred vision or seeing the surroundings as surreal and dreamlike, sometimes with mild hallucinations that can be vivid yet not entirely immersive. Thought processes can undergo significant changes under the influence of dissociative psychedelics. Individuals may find their usual patterns of thinking disrupted, leading to a state where thoughts seem fragmented or slowed down (Clingo J. 2024). Ketamine can create space for new perspectives to emerge, allowing one to consider personal issues or memories without the usual emotional responses (Fattore et al. 2018). In therapeutic settings, this detachment can help individuals approach traumatic experiences with less distress, potentially facilitating healing and understanding.

Shifts in emotional states are also noteworthy from a psychotherapeutic standpoint. Some people may experience a sense of calmness, peace, or even euphoria, finding temporary relief from anxiety or depressive feelings. This emotional neutrality or uplift can provide a valuable contrast to one's typical mood, offering insights into different ways of feeling and relating to others. It is important to note that PCP and DXM have not been studied in the context of psychotherapy and that they carry risks of harm. And although DXM has medical use as a cough suppressant, PCP is not currently used as a medicine.

## HEALTH RISKS OF DISSOCIATIVE PSYCHEDELICS

Dissociative psychedelics such as ketamine, DXM, and PCP come with their own set of risks (Huang and Lin 2020; Gershman and Fass 2013). Unlike classic psychedelics, these substances can lead to psychological dependence and, in some cases, withdrawal symptoms, particularly with prolonged or heavy use. They have a higher potential for abuse compared to classic psychedelics. Physiologically, these drugs can significantly impact the body, including elevated heart rate and blood pressure, nausea, vomiting, and impaired motor function. Users may also experience paranoia, confusion, and disorientation during use. Psychological effects can be intense, with some individuals experiencing severe agitation (Dominici et al. 2015). Long-term use, especially of ketamine and PCP, can lead to cognitive impairment and memory loss. Ketamine can cause urinary tract problems known as ketamine-induced cystitis (Zhou et al. 2023). While flashbacks and persistent perceptual disturbances are less common with dissociative psychedelics, some users may experience lingering psychological or perceptual issues that interfere with daily functioning. It's important to recognize that dissociative psychedelics carry significant risks, and their use can result in both immediate and long-term health consequences.

# Empathogens

Also referred to as entactogens or entheogens (Stocker and Liechti 2024), these substances are known for their ability to enhance feelings of empathy, emotional openness, and interconnectedness. The most well-known substances in this category are MDMA and MDEA.

The primary feature of empathogens is their ability to increase serotonin levels in the brain. Users typically experience heightened emotions, increased empathy and sociability, mild euphoria, and sometimes mild sensory enhancement. An example of mild sensory enhancement would be that those under the influence of an empathogen may feel increased pleasure while dancing to music or receiving a hug.

There is growing interest in the therapeutic potential of MDMA, particularly in the treatment of PTSD and other mental health disorders (Danforth et al. 2018; Nicholas et al. 2022). Its ability to enhance emotional openness is seen as potentially beneficial in psychotherapy settings.

## *MDMA*

*Chemical structure:* MDMA is a synthetic compound and a member of the **substituted methylene-dioxyphenethylamine** and **substituted amphetamine** classes. Structurally, it is similar to both amphetamine and mescaline, with a **methylenedioxy group** attached to the **aromatic ring**.

*Pharmacology:* MDMA's primary action is to increase the release of the neurotransmitters serotonin, dopamine, and **norepinephrine**. It also has a significant effect on the release and reuptake of serotonin, leading to a surge in serotonin level, and a mild stimulant effect due to its impact on dopamine and norepinephrine.

*Effects:* This action results in a lift in mood and an increase in feelings of empathy for others. MDMA also often creates feelings of safety, closeness with others, and enhanced trust in relationships, all properties that are of interest in psychotherapeutic uses.

Here is a statement from a research participant that describes the experience of MDMA:

"I think that the MDMA gave me the ability to feel as though I was capable and safe of tackling the issues. Whereas before I feared those thoughts and I tried to avoid them at all times, and avoid things that reminded me of those thoughts, I think it allowed me to feel safe in my space. Of being able to fight it. I felt like I had the ability and tools, whereas before I was unarmed, unarmored, and had no support" (Barone et al. 2019).

## MDEA

*Chemical structure:* MDEA is structurally similar to MDMA, differing only in the length of its **alpha-alkyl chain**. It is also a member of the substituted methylenedioxyphenethylamine and substituted amphetamine classes.

*Pharmacology:* MDEA acts similarly to MDMA. Like MDMA, it increases the release of neurotransmitters, particularly serotonin, and to a lesser extent dopamine and norepinephrine.

*Effects:* While it is not as strong of a mood lifter as MDMA, MDEA seems to increase empathy more.

Empathogens foster an enhanced sense of emotional connectedness (Stocker and Liechti 2024) and empathy (Hysek et al. 2014) towards others. Users often experience enhanced feelings of trust, openness (Wagner et al. 2017), and closeness, which can lead to deeper social interactions and a heightened appreciation for relationships, although these perceptions may not always be accurate (Bedi, Hyman, and de Wit 2010). Sensory perceptions may become more vivid, with music sounding richer and tactile sensations feeling more pleasurable (Bershad et al. 2019). Visual enhancements are also common, with lights appearing brighter and colors more intense, although full hallucinations are less common than with classic psychedelics. Individuals may find it easier to access and express their feelings, often articulating thoughts that are usually difficult to convey. This emotional openness can facilitate personal insights and breakthroughs, allowing one to address personal issues or traumas with increased compassion and understanding (Mitchell et al. 2023). In therapeutic settings, this heightened empathy and reduced fear response can help individuals process difficult emotions, potentially aiding in healing and personal growth (Gorman et al. 2020). Shifts in emotional states are a hallmark of empathogens from a psychotherapeutic perspective. Many people report feelings of euphoria, warmth, and overall well-being, alongside a reduction in anxiety and negative thought patterns.

## HEALTH RISKS OF EMPATHOGENS

It's important to note that while substances like MDMA have shown promise in clinical research for conditions such as PTSD, they also carry risks. Potential adverse effects include dehydration, overheating, and negative mood changes in the days following use, sometimes referred to as a "comedown." Risks of these substances also include neurotoxicity (nerve damage), especially with repeated high doses, and the potential for adverse cardiovascular effects (causing harm to the heart). These risks are mainly associated with recreational use, as the clinical environment includes careful screening, precise dosing, and a controlled, pure supply of the drug. Additionally, unregulated use of empathogens can lead to exposure to **adulterated** substances, increasing the risk of harm. Outside of clinical settings, the purity and composition of what is sold as MDMA can vary and sometimes include harmful substances, further elevating the potential for adverse effects.

## Atypical Psychedelics

Atypical psychedelics are a diverse group of psychoactive substances that don't fit neatly into the classic psychedelic, dissociative, or empathogen categories. They often have unique chemical structures and pharmacological profiles. We've included ayahuasca in this category because it combines the properties of several psychoactive plants. Two other notable examples are *Salvia divinorum* and ibogaine. Finally, *Amanita muscaria* mushrooms have a unique set of effects and risks worth mentioning.

### *AYAHUASCA*

*Chemical structure:* Ayahuasca is a traditional Amazonian brew made by combining two primary plants, *Banisteriopsis caapi* (a vine) and *Psychotria viridis* (a shrub). *B. caapi* contains **harmala alkaloids** such as harmine, harmaline, and tetrahydroharmine, which are **beta-carbolines** and **monoamine oxidase A** (MAO-A) inhibitors. *P. viridis* provides DMT, a potent psychedelic.

*Pharmacology:* The harmala alkaloids in *B. caapi* inhibit the MAO-A enzyme in the gut and liver. This enzyme normally breaks down DMT, rendering it inactive when taken orally. When MAO-A is inhibited, DMT can enter the bloodstream and cross the blood-brain barrier. DMT primarily acts as an agonist at serotonin 5-HT2A receptors, leading to its psychoactive effects. The combination of MAO-A inhibition and DMT activity results in ayahuasca's unique and profound psychoactive profile.

*Effects:* Ayahuasca induces significant alterations in consciousness, including intense visual and auditory hallucinations, enhanced introspection, and deep emotional and spiritual experiences. The effects can last several hours and are sometimes accompanied by physical reactions such as nausea and vomiting, which are traditionally considered part of a cleansing process. Ayahuasca has been studied for potential therapeutic benefits in treating conditions like depression and substance use disorders.

# About Ayahuasca

We've listed ayahuasca as an atypical psychedelic, but this complex, traditional Amazonian brew defies easy categorization. Ayahuasca has roots in indigenous communities in South America, including traditional use in present-day Peru, Ecuador, and Brazil. Traditionally prepared by a shaman over the course of days, ayahuasca includes plants that contain DMT and other naturally occurring compounds that mix with the DMT, making it psychoactive when consumed orally. The mixture can also include a variety of other plants specific to the local culture or the specific reason for which it is prepared. Researchers have documented that regular use of ayahuasca doesn't result in addiction (Grob et al. 1996) and has potential as a treatment for depression and alcohol use problems (Bouso and Riba 2014; Palhano-Fontes et al. 2022).

Ayahuasca has recently become popular in North America and Europe among people with no historical connection to indigenous use in South America. These people seek it for spiritual and emotional healing, personal growth, psychological struggles, and a variety of health concerns (Winkelman 2005; Kavenská and Simonová 2015). While there is generally a well-intentioned exchange of traditional practitioners who share and provide ayahuasca to those from other communities, there have also been instances of exploitation and abuse. The implications for local communities are enormous, and the disconnect between indigenous belief systems and those of visitors to these communities can result in additional challenges for integration (Gearin 2022). We encourage anyone interested in ayahuasca to research it thoroughly. We've provided additional resources in the resource list to help.

## SALVIA DIVINORUM

*Chemical structure:* The primary active compound in *S. divinorum* is Salvinorin A, a **diterpenoid**. This compound is unique among psychoactive substances because it contains no nitrogen atoms, distinguishing it from other psychedelics, which are typically alkaloids and contain at least one nitrogen atom.

*Pharmacology:* Salvinorin A's primary action is as a potent **kappa opioid receptor agonist**. Unlike most other psychedelics, it does not affect serotonin. Instead, Salvinorin A has distinctive dissociative and hallucinogenic effects.

*Effects:* The effects of *S. divinorum* are typically short-lived but intense, including altered visual perceptions, feelings of traveling through time and space, and changes in sensory and environmental perception similar to those of classic psychedelics (Johnson et al. 2011).

## IBOGAINE

*Chemical structure:* Ibogaine is a naturally occurring psychoactive compound found in the roots of the African shrub *Tabernanthe iboga*. Chemically, it is similar to other classic psychedelics like DMT and psilocybin.

*Pharmacology:* Ibogaine is unique in its broad pharmacological profile. It interacts with multiple neurotransmitter systems, including acting as an agonist at serotonin receptors and an antagonist at NMDA receptors. It also affects other targets, such as **opioid receptors** and **acetylcholine receptors**.

*Effects:* Its most notable effect is its potential to reduce withdrawal symptoms and cravings in opioid addiction, though it also induces a profound, introspective psychedelic experience (Schenberg et al. 2014; Brown and Alper 2018).

## AMANITA MUSCARIA

*Chemical structure:* The main psychoactive compounds in the *A. muscaria* mushroom family are muscimol and ibotenic acid (a prodrug of muscimol). Muscimol is an agonist for **gamma-amino-butyric acid (GABA) receptors** (Rivera-Illanes and Recabarren-Gajardo 2024).

*Pharmacology:* Muscimol mimics GABA, an inhibitory neurotransmitter, making neurons in the CNS less excitable.

*Effects:* Muscimol has sedative-hypnotic, depressant, and psychedelic effects. It has been studied for use in treating migraines, epilepsy, pain, and cerebral ischemia (stroke).

Unlike classic psychedelics, which primarily act on the serotonin system, atypical psychedelics have varied mechanisms of action, affecting a range of neurotransmitter systems. The effects of atypical psychedelics can differ significantly from those of classic psychedelics, often inducing unique subjective experiences. As noted above, *S, divinorum* can produce very intense, short-lived dissociative states, while ibogaine can trigger long-lasting introspective experiences.

Some atypical psychedelics are being researched for their potential therapeutic uses, such as ibogaine for addiction treatment. However, their broader pharmacological effects and safety profiles require careful consideration. The legal status of atypical psychedelics varies widely, with many being subject to research restrictions.

Atypical psychedelics offer a fascinating area of study due to their unique effects and mechanisms of action. Their potential therapeutic applications, particularly in areas not addressed by other psychoactive substances, make them a subject of ongoing scientific interest.

### HEALTH RISKS OF ATYPICAL PSYCHEDELICS

It's important to note that while substances like *S. divinorum*, ibogaine, *A. muscaria*, and ayahuasca have been used in traditional practices and are being explored in clinical research for their potential therapeutic benefits, they also carry significant risks. These substances are very different in their effects and mechanisms of action, but all can produce intense and unpredictable experiences. Potential adverse effects include nausea, vomiting, confusion, and in some cases, severe psychological distress or psychosis. Ibogaine, for instance, can cause a delay in the relaxation of the heart following a heartbeat. This can lead to an irregular heartbeat, which can cause fainting, seizures, or sudden death (Litjens and Brunt 2016). *A. muscaria* contains toxic compounds that, if not properly prepared, can cause delirium, seizures, and other dangerous symptoms. *S. divinorum* can induce profound but short-lived hallucinations and dissociative states, which may be distressing or disorienting. Ayahuasca often leads to intense emotional and psychological experiences that can be overwhelming without proper guidance.

## Legal Status and Implications

The possession, sale, and use of psychedelics are regulated under various laws in different countries. In this book, we provide information based on the legal status in the United States at the time of writing. Regardless of where you live, you should check your national and any local regulatory agencies for updated information.

Regulations in the United States adopted a scheduling system under the Controlled Substances Act in 1971. This law replaced the Marijuana Tax Act and other earlier laws that regulated the use of opiates. The most restricted category of drugs is Schedule I; these are drugs that are defined by the DEA as having no accepted medical use and a high potential for abuse. They can't be prescribed by doctors for any medical condition. While there is some evidence that some of the drugs currently listed as Schedule I have some medical use and low potential for abuse, getting the government to reconsider and move them to a lower restriction category is an extensive process.

However, researchers have been able to get permission to use Schedule I drugs in research studies. At first researchers could only study their use in healthy volunteers (Strassman, Qualls, and Berg 1996), but later won permission to study their use in people who suffer from mental health issues. This shift, which took place starting in the early 90s, recognizes the potential for a different way of thinking about psychedelics—as valuable medicines instead of addictive drugs to be avoided.

Schedule II and III drugs are available by prescription and some—for example, ketamine—are used as an **off-label** treatment for mental health conditions. Off-label refers to a scenario in which something is usually prescribed for a specific use, but doctors are allowed to prescribe it for something else. For example, ketamine is an **anesthetic**, but doctors can choose to prescribe it for depression.

As of January 2024, the DEA classifies all the classic psychedelics we've mentioned here as Schedule I, along with MDMA, MDEA, and ibogaine. While mescaline is included in this group, certain Native American tribes are permitted to use peyote in religious ceremonies. Ketamine and PCP are on Schedule II. DXM is legal when used as directed in over-the-counter cough medicines. *S. divinorum* is not regulated by the DEA, but some states do have laws concerning it.

## Decriminalization, Deprioritization, and State-Level Regulation

To complicate matters further, there are a number of cities and states that have **decriminalized** or **deprioritized** psychedelics in the last few years (for example, Denver, Colorado, in 2019 and Oregon in 2020). The trend toward such measures continues. The result is a patchwork of policies that may imply that use is safe and acceptable. This may increase risk through lack of regulations, especially when it comes to the issue of a safe supply.

- **Deprioritization** refers to a policy in which law enforcement agencies are instructed to treat the enforcement of laws against certain drug offenses as a low priority. This means that while the drug remains illegal, the police and judicial system will typically not target or prosecute individuals for possession or use of small quantities of the drug.

- **Decriminalization** refers to the reduction or removal of criminal penalties for certain drug offenses, usually possession of small quantities for personal use. Under decriminalization, these offenses are typically reclassified as civil violations, similar to parking violations, or may carry no penalty at all.

As you may imagine, deprioritization is easier to achieve and implement than decriminalization. However, decriminalization has a broader impact on the stigma and consequences associated with drug possession and use. For example, if someone were to be caught by the local police for another crime—robbery, for example—while in possession of a deprioritized but not decriminalized drug, prosecutors could add on charges for the possession of that drug. While the police aren't out looking for it, it is fair game if found in connection with something else. If the drug was decriminalized, the individual would be protected from charges linked to possession. A further complication is that either of these approaches may be implemented on a state level while the possession and sale of the same drug carries criminal penalties at the federal level. In that case, if the case becomes a federal one, the federal government could charge possession even though the drug was decriminalized by the state. Be aware that even if you live in an area that has locally deprioritized or decriminalized psychedelics, the federal government's stance has not changed.

Another form of policy change is state level regulation and licensing of psychedelics; for example, Oregon's Measure 109. This legislation, passed by a ballot measure in 2020, establishes that the state shall license psilocybin producers, facilitators, and service centers where people can receive psilocybin under a **supervised adult use** model. This is different from a dispensary model that is common in states that have **legalized** cannabis, licensed dispensaries, and allowed cannabis users—whether for medical or personal reasons—to buy and use cannabis at home. Although the regulatory authority in Oregon is the Oregon Health Authority, psilocybin services cannot be offered as treatment for any health condition, and psilocybin cannot be sold for consumption outside of licensed service centers*. That said, people who do suffer from health conditions—mental health or otherwise—may access these services and may benefit. This creates a new system that is outside of the medical model, yet with the assurance of a safe supply and professional providers. It also bears mentioning that Colorado has passed the Natural Medicine Health Act, which makes psilocybin services available in Colorado with a similar but less restrictive set of rules. Other states are looking to implement similar programs in the coming years.

But as noted, the federal government's stance has not changed. Psilocybin producers, providers, and those accessing services must be aware that their activities are prohibited by federal law. Even if DEA agents don't arrest and prosecute anyone for these activities, the situation is complicated. For one thing, those providing psilocybin services face restrictions on their use of federally insured banks and can have difficulty obtaining business insurance. People who are court-involved, have pending legal matters, or who are involved in custody disputes may not be protected from consequences should they choose to participate in psilocybin services.

The following exercise may help you become more aware of the legal situation where you live.

---

\*       At the time of writing, this is being challenged in court because it excludes access by homebound individuals and conflicts with the Americans with Disabilities Act.

# Exploring the Legal Status of Psychedelics in Your Area

**Objective:** The goal of this exercise is to increase your awareness of the current legal status of various psychedelics in your area. Having this information is essential for informed decision-making in the context of psychedelic therapy and harm reduction, whether you are a therapist or potential user.

**Instructions:** Find reputable sources online to identify the legal status of psychedelics in your country or state. Look for the key terms *decriminalized*, *deprioritized*, *legalized*, and **medicalized**. Remember, the legal status can vary significantly for different substances.

Use the table below to document your findings. Be specific about which substances are affected by these laws and any relevant details (like allowed quantities, medical prerequisites, etc.). Remember, legal statuses can change. Plan a periodic review (perhaps every six months) to stay informed about any legal changes regarding psychedelics in your state.

| Psychedelic Substance | Decriminalized | Deprioritized | Legalized | Medicalized | Notes |
|---|---|---|---|---|---|
| Psilocybin | Yes/No | Yes/No | Yes/No | Yes/No | [Any specific details] |
|  |  |  |  |  |  |
|  |  |  |  |  |  |
|  |  |  |  |  |  |

**Reflection Questions:** Write down your answers to each of the following questions. Spending some time thinking about these will help you understand the rationale for your choices, and the choices others may be making that might affect you.

- How does the legal status in your area impact the use of psychedelics in therapeutic settings?

- How do your personal views align with or differ from the current legal perspective in your state?

- Considering the legality, what are the ethical considerations for yourself as a psychedelic user or a therapist?

_____

_____

_____

_____

_____

_____

_____

If you are a psychedelic user, discuss your findings and reflections with your therapist or a trusted friend. If you are a therapist, consider discussing these points in a peer supervision group or with a colleague to broaden your understanding.

We've reviewed a wealth of information about psychedelics in this chapter! We started with the basic categories of psychedelics, moved on to chemistry and pharmacology, and covered the legal status at both the federal and state level. You now have a rich basis on which to make decisions about psychedelics for yourself. Remember that all choices are individual. What feels risky for you can feel safe and comfortable for someone else. We hope the exercises in this chapter helped you see the relevance of this information to your personal situation and helped you identify your personal comfort level with psychedelics.

# CHAPTER 4

# Preparation

Good preparation is the key to reducing the likelihood of negative psychedelic experiences and increasing the benefits of integration (McCartney, McGovern, and De Foe 2023). As with traveling, preparation for a psychedelic experience should include safety planning and gathering the things you can reasonably expect to need along the way. This includes both material items and internal resources like breathing exercises. At the same time, part of the allure is always the unexpected. Good preparation will help you be open to what actually arises in the moment.

This chapter provides you with activities for developing a good mindset prior to a psychedelic experience. We share common safety protocols used in clinical trials to address difficult psychedelic experiences if they arise. We also provide tools for learning emotional regulation skills that can be useful both during and after a psychedelic experience.

During the preparation phase, expectations for the psychedelic experience itself, as well as the outcomes, can be very high. Working with your expectations will be of benefit as you integrate your experience. We start by discussing the concept of inner healing intelligence, which leads into the ideas of the **inner-directed experience**, the **unfolding process**, and **nonlinear change**. The more prepared you are, the less likely that you will be caught off guard by what is occurring.

# Understanding Inner Healing Intelligence

The concept of inner healing intelligence might sound unfamiliar or even a bit mystical, but this idea plays a key role in how many people approach psychedelic therapy (O'Donnell et al. 2024). First introduced by Czech psychiatrist Stanislav Grof and influenced by the work of pioneering psychoanalyst Carl Jung ("Interview with Dr. Stanislav Grof" 2007), inner healing intelligence refers to the belief that each person has an innate ability to heal and grow from within. Think of it as the mind's natural capacity to heal itself, much like how the body heals a wound without us needing to direct the process. Under the right conditions—what we call set and setting—this inner capacity can be accessed and amplified, especially with the help of psychedelics.

For those looking to engage in a psychedelic experience, it's important to know that inner healing intelligence isn't a magic cure. Just as the body has limits, like being unable to regenerate a missing limb, the mind's ability to heal doesn't guarantee all problems will be resolved. However, this concept offers a powerful framework for working through deep emotional challenges, such as processing trauma (M. Mithoefer 2013) or coming to terms with life circumstances that can't be changed, like a terminal diagnosis (Becker 2022).

If you're considering psychedelic therapy, remember that you already hold wisdom and insight within yourself. The role of a guide, facilitator, or therapist is not to tell you what your inner healing looks like, but to support you as you explore this process for yourself. In fact, one of the most important aspects of inner healing intelligence is that it centers you as the expert of your own life. This approach empowers you to listen to your emotions, thoughts, and experiences and find meaning and healing in your way.

This can be liberating, but it also requires a strong emphasis on safety. As the individual in the psychedelic experience, your **autonomy**—your ability to make decisions for yourself—must always be respected. At no point should a therapist or guide impose their views or try to direct your experience, except to ensure your physical safety. This is why creating a safe, supportive, and respectful environment is so crucial. During a psychedelic session, you may be more vulnerable to suggestion or influence, so it's essential that the people around you respect your space and decisions. If you're undergoing therapy with a guide or therapist, ensure that your autonomy is held as a priority.

It's also important to know that the term "inner healing intelligence" doesn't have to resonate with everyone. Some people may prefer other terms like inner wisdom, intuition, or personal **agency**. Others might relate this concept to therapeutic ideas like psychological flexibility, from the therapeutic school known as acceptance and commitment therapy (ACT), or intrinsic motivation as used in Motivational Interviewing. No matter what you call it, the core idea remains the same: healing and growth come from within, and your sense of personal integrity is an essential part of the process. It's crucial to approach the concept of inner healing intelligence with humility and respect. The therapeutic space should be one of support, not control, because while psychedelics can open people up to deep insights, this can make them vulnerable.

# Inner-Directed Experience

In psychedelic therapy, to facilitate connection with one's inner healing capacity, the inner-directed approach is used. This means that individuals are encouraged to turn their attention inward, exploring their own thoughts, emotions, and memories while under the influence of psychedelics. The introspective journey can unveil deep-seated insights and emotional truths, facilitating profound healing and personal growth. Unlike traditional talk therapies that rely heavily on verbal communication with a therapist, psychedelic therapy using inner-directed experience emphasizes the individual's personal encounters and revelations. This form of therapy is known for promoting a transformative inner awakening that can go a long way toward healing mental and emotional distress.

# The Unfolding Process

The concept of the unfolding process, attributed to transpersonal psychologist John Welwood (1984), is a cornerstone of our understanding of psychological healing and spiritual growth through psychedelic therapy. It refers to the spontaneous personal and spiritual growth that can occur naturally when individuals engage deeply with their inner experiences. Welwood posits that by embracing our innermost feelings, thoughts, and sensations without judgment or resistance, we enable a process of unfolding. This unfolding reveals deeper layers of our psyche and spirit, leading to insights and transformations that are not forced but emerge organically. The process is akin to a flower naturally blooming. Each individual's unique path of growth and healing unfolds in its own time and manner, guided by one's innate wisdom.

# Nonlinear Change

Nonlinear change, in the context of psychedelic therapy, refers to unpredictable and often profound shifts in understanding, perception, and emotional processing that can occur during and after a psychedelic experience. Unlike the gradual and predictable progression seen in other forms of therapy, changes facilitated by psychedelics can be sudden, deep, and transformative, occurring in ways that are not straightforward or predictable. This concept acknowledges that healing and psychological growth do not always follow a linear trajectory. In other words, this growth does not occur in predictable steps. Instead, significant breakthroughs and insights can emerge abruptly, leading to rapid shifts in a person's mental state, behavior, and overall well-being. Such nonlinear changes can result in lasting improvements in various mental health conditions while fostering a deeper sense of connection, meaning, and self-awareness.

With these concepts in mind, you can prepare and be ready for whatever may arise during and after your experience. The following exercises take you through some key aspects of preparation. Notice which exercises feel less appealing to you. Maybe you feel as though you are already prepared in certain areas and don't need to do any further work. That may be the case. But you might ask yourself if you're avoiding an exercise because it feels too challenging. We encourage you to take a look at all of the areas of preparation covered in this chapter. We want you to be as prepared as possible going into your psychedelic experience.

## Rehearsing Emotion Regulation

**Objective:** To practice and strengthen emotion regulation skills in preparation for managing challenging emotions that may arise during a psychedelic experience.

**Instructions:**

1.  Identify a recent, mildly emotionally challenging situation you experienced. It could be a time when you felt some anxiety, sadness, anger, or another difficult emotion. Do not choose an overwhelming or traumatic experience. Describe the situation:

    _____

    _____

    _____

| | |
|---|---|
| What specific emotions did you feel? | |
| Rate the intensity of each emotion from 1 to 10, with 10 being the most intense. | |
| What physical sensations and urges accompanied each emotion? | |
| What thoughts or judgments arose? | |

2.  Now, close your eyes and visualize this situation in detail, as if you are back in that moment. Allow yourself to reexperience the emotions, thoughts, sensations and urges that arise.

3.  When you reach a 4–6 level of emotion, open your eyes and immediately begin practicing the following emotion regulation skills for at least five minutes:

    _Take slow, deep breaths, focusing your attention on the sensations of the breath entering and leaving your body. Count your exhales up to 10._

    _Mentally note and label the specific emotions you are feeling. For example, "I'm feeling anxious right now. This is anxiety."_

*Visualize the emotions as waves that rise up, crest, and pass. Imagine yourself riding the waves without fighting them or getting pulled under. The waves will eventually subside on their own.*

*If judgments or distressing thoughts arise, notice them and imagine them floating away like leaves on a stream, without engaging with their content. Gently return your focus to your breath.*

*Offer yourself compassion and validation. For example, you can tell yourself "This emotion is intense, but I can handle it. It's okay and understandable to feel this way sometimes."*

4.  After at least five minutes of practicing these skills, check in with yourself. How intense are the emotions now on a scale of 0–10? If they have decreased to a manageable level, take a few more deep breaths and slowly open your eyes. If the emotions are still higher than a 4, continue the regulation skills exercise a bit longer.

5.  Reflect on the experience. What was it like to allow the emotions to rise up and approach them with mindfulness rather than fighting them? Which specific skills were most helpful? Write down any insights.

_____

_____

_____

_____

_____

6.  Repeat this visualization and skill rehearsal process several times using the same memory. Notice if it gradually becomes easier to regulate your emotions. Then practice with other emotionally charged memories. The more you rehearse these skills while in an activated emotional state, the more effectively you will be able to use them during a psychedelic experience if challenging emotions arise.

Remind yourself that emotions during a psychedelic experience, even very intense ones, are temporary and will pass. You can ride the waves of emotion without getting pulled under. Breathe, label, and offer compassion to whatever arises.

By rehearsing emotion regulation skills in this way, you are training yourself to have a skillful mindful response rather than being overwhelmed when strong emotions surface. You are building confidence in your capacity to navigate choppy emotional waters. With practice, you can enter a psychedelic experience equipped with tools to stay anchored, working with your emotions rather than against them.

Therapeutic touch can be a valuable tool in psychedelic experiences, offering support and grounding during intense emotional experiences. However, it's essential that touch is only used with clear consent and respect for a person's boundaries. This exercise will help you explore your comfort levels and communicate your needs around touch.

## Exploring Comfort and Consent with Touch in Psychedelic Therapy

**Objective:** To establish clear preferences and boundaries around therapeutic and safety touch, and practice communicating these needs before a psychedelic therapy session.

**Instructions:** Take a few moments to reflect on your personal history and relationship with touch. Consider these questions and write down any insights or important points you want to share.

- What have been your experiences with touch in therapeutic or healing contexts?

- Are there certain types of touch that feel particularly comforting or soothing to you?

- Are there any forms of touch that you're uncomfortable with or want to avoid?

- How do you typically communicate your touch preferences to others?

_____

_____

_____

_____

_____

In psychedelic experiences, we use the principle of "double consent" for touch. This means getting your consent both before the session (when you're not under the influence of any substances) and again in the moment if the need for touch arises. Reflect on these consent and boundary considerations, and note your preferences and any key points you want to discuss.

- What specific types of touch, if any, are you comfortable receiving (hand holding, hand on shoulder, gentle grasp on forearm)?

- Are there any areas of your body that are off-limits for touch?

- How would you like to ask for consent to touch in the moment (verbal question, visual cue, waiting for you to initiate)?

- How will you communicate if you want the touch to stop (verbal cue, gently pull away)?

- Safety touch refers to physical support for ensuring your well-being, such as steadying you if you are walking and may fall. Will you provide consent to this form of touch?

_____

_____

_____

_____

_____

Take time with your therapist or facilitator to discuss your reflections and preferences around therapeutic and safety touch. Remember, you have the right to withdraw your consent at any time. Some key points to cover:

- All forms of touch conducted with respect and without any sexual intent

- Your overall comfort level and boundaries with touch

- Specific types of touch you are okay with or want to avoid

- How you'll give consent for touch during the session

- How you'll communicate if you want touch to stop

- Any concerns or questions you have about the use of touch

If you feel comfortable, practice receiving touch to help build your confidence and comfort in communicating about touch. This could involve:

- Your facilitator placing a hand on your shoulder or offering their hand for you to hold

- Giving a verbal or nonverbal cue to initiate touch

- Cues for when you want the touch to end

**Closing Reflection**

Take a moment to check in with yourself after this exploration and practice. How are you feeling? What did you learn about your preferences and boundaries around touch? Is there anything else you want to discuss?

_____

_____

_____

_____

_____

Remember, open communication and trust are essential for safe and effective use of touch.

The next exercise is about normalizing nonordinary states and framing meaning-making as an ongoing process.

# Embracing the Unknowable

**Objective:** To help develop comfort with experiences that may be difficult to understand or articulate during the psychedelic journey.

**Instructions:**

1.  Think back to a time when you encountered something extraordinary, profound, or mysterious that was challenging to express in words. This could be a dream, a work of art, a spiritual or emotional experience, or a moment in nature. Spend a few minutes writing about this experience in as much detail as you can recall.

_____

_____

_____

_____

2.  Now, imagine you must explain this experience to someone who has never encountered anything like it. Write a paragraph attempting to convey the essence of the experience. Notice any points where you struggle to find the right words or feel like you're not quite capturing the depth of the experience. Reflect on the following questions:

    o   What aspects of the experience were easiest to describe? What was most challenging?

    o   How did it feel to try to put this ineffable experience into words?

    o   Did the process of articulating the experience change your perception or memory of it in any way?

    o   What, if anything, remained unspoken or unexpressed in your description? Is there a nonverbal way to express this experience, perhaps through sound, visual art, or movement?

    _____

    _____

    _____

    _____

    _____

3.  During your psychedelic journey, you may encounter states of consciousness, insights, or sensations that similarly resist easy explanation or understanding. You may experience realities that don't fit neatly into your existing frameworks of meaning. How do you feel about this?

4.  On a separate sheet of paper, write a letter to yourself to read prior to your psychedelic session. In this letter, offer yourself permission to encounter the unknowable, the ineffable, the mysterious. Remind yourself that it's natural and even expected to have experiences that defy immediate understanding or articulation. Encourage yourself to greet these experiences with openness, curiosity, and patience, trusting that meaning will unfold in its own time.

5.  Create a list of supportive statements or affirmations that you can refer to during your psychedelic session if you find yourself grasping for understanding or struggling to make sense of your experience. Some examples might include:

    o   I embrace experiences that are beyond my current understanding.

    o   I allow my experiences to be as they are, without needing to control or define them.

    o   I trust in the wisdom of my journey, even if its meaning is not immediately clear.

o    I am open to new ways of perceiving and understanding.

_____

_____

_____

_____

_____

_____

6.   Discuss how you might navigate experiences that feel ineffable or challenging to understand during your psychedelic session. What resources or reminders might be helpful? How can you cultivate a sense of trust and openness in the face of the unknown?

_____

_____

_____

_____

_____

_____

This exercise can help you practice psychological flexibility and build resilience in the face of experiences that may not fit your existing models of reality. You're learning to let go of the need for immediate understanding and instead, cultivate a sense of openness and curiosity toward the vast landscape of human experience. This skillset will serve you well as you navigate the uncharted territories of your psychedelic journey, allowing you to be present with what arises and trust in the ongoing process of meaning-making. Please keep in mind that psychological flexibility doesn't mean accepting whatever arises as truth.

The next exercise draws on relational elements to strengthen the therapeutic alliance.

# Building a Collaborative Partnership with Your Psychedelic Facilitator

**Objective:** To clarify roles, responsibilities, and ways the facilitator can support you during the psychedelic session. This exercise aims to foster trust and a sense of collaborative partnership.

**Instructions:**

1.  Reflect on your previous experiences with healthcare providers, therapists, or other supportive figures. Make a list of qualities or actions that helped you feel safe, understood, and supported in those relationships. For example, perhaps they were excellent listeners, were nonjudgmental, or provided clear explanations.

    _____

    _____

    _____

    _____

    _____

    _____

    _____

2.  Now, consider your upcoming psychedelic session. What specific qualities or actions from your facilitator would help you feel most safe, supported, and able to fully engage in the experience? Write these down. Examples might include maintaining a calm presence, offering gentle guidance, or providing reassurance during challenging moments.

    _____

    _____

    _____

    _____

    _____

    _____

3.  Review the list of your preferences and needs. Circle the top 3–5 that feel most important to you in the context of your psychedelic session. These are your key needs for feeling safe and supported in this work.

4.  Now, imagine you are the facilitator. Write a short paragraph describing your understanding of your role and responsibilities in supporting someone through a psychedelic experience. What do you see as the most important aspects of your job? How will you ensure your client feels safe, respected, and supported throughout the process?

5.  Reflect on the following questions:

    o   What similarities or differences do you notice between your key needs and your description of the facilitator's role?

    o   How might you and your facilitator work together to ensure these needs are met?

    o   What else does your facilitator need to know about you and your preferences to best support you?

    o   What questions do you have for your facilitator about their approach or the process of the session?

    _____

    _____

    _____

    _____

    _____

    _____

    _____

    _____

6.  Draft notes for an in-person conversation. Share your reflections from this exercise, including:

    o   Your key needs for feeling safe and supported during the session

    o   Your understanding of the facilitator's role and how you can work together

    o   Any additional information about yourself that would be helpful for them to know o     Questions you have about the process or their approach

_____

_____

_____

_____

_____

_____

7.   Bring your notes to your next meeting with your facilitator. Use this as a starting point for a collaborative discussion about how you can work together to create the most supportive and effective experience possible. Be open to your facilitator's perspective and suggestions, while also advocating for your own needs.

By proactively communicating your needs, understanding your facilitator's role, and co-creating agreements for your work together, you are laying the groundwork for a strong, trusting, and supportive partnership. This relational foundation will allow you to more fully engage in the transformative potential of the psychedelic experience, knowing that you have a skilled and caring ally by your side. Remember, your facilitator is there to support you and to help create the conditions for your own innate healing wisdom to emerge.

Now that you've covered the psychological and emotional aspects of preparation, the following checklist covers the logistics of what you need to establish the safest possible container for your experience. Remember that safety is relative: one person's risk tolerance or individual risk profile might be very different from another's. If you are planning a psychedelic experience with friends, be sure to assess your own needs and make choices based on what works for you.

# The Container

The following steps will help you create a safe container for your psychedelic experience.

1. **Research and choose the substance:** Make sure you understand the effects, duration, and legality of the psychedelic you plan to use. Different substances offer different experiences and require different preparations.

2. **Check physical health:** Ensure that you are in good physical health. You may wish to consult a healthcare professional, especially if you have underlying health conditions or are taking medication that could interact with the psychedelic.

3. **Secure a safe setting:** Choose a comfortable, familiar, and safe environment where you won't be disturbed. The setting can significantly influence your experience.

4. **Arrange for a sitter:** Have a trusted, sober person present who can assist if needed. This person should be experienced or knowledgeable about psychedelics and their effects. If you are at a festival or other event, be sure you know where to find harm reduction services ahead of time.

5. **Prepare supplies:** Gather necessary supplies, including water, snacks, comfortable clothing, and blankets. Consider having items that can help ground you, like familiar objects.

6. **Plan the timing:** Ensure that you have enough time for the experience, including the peak and comedown periods. Avoid having obligations immediately after the experience.

7. **Inform a contact:** Let someone know about your plans, especially if they won't be physically present. Share your location and how long you expect the experience to last.

8. **Dietary considerations:** Some recommend fasting or following specific dietary guidelines before the experience to reduce nausea or enhance the experience. For example, tyramine-rich foods can interact with the monoamine oxidase inhibitor in ayahuasca and lead to a sudden and dangerous increase in blood pressure.

9. **Emergency plan:** Have a plan in case of an unexpected adverse reaction. This includes knowing the local emergency numbers and having a way to reach help if needed.

10. **Post-experience rest:** Ensure that you have a day or more to rest, process, and integrate the experience without the pressure of work or social obligations.

# CHAPTER 5

# The Trip—Intentions, Attitudes, and Expectations

Now that you've prepared yourself psychologically and arranged for your psychedelic experience to be as safe as possible, let's turn our attention to a few key principles to keep in mind during the actual experience. The goal is to be able to relax into the experience, remaining flexible yet stable no matter what happens.

This chapter will introduce you to some methods for navigating a difficult psychedelic experience and empower you to work with and integrate experiences that may feel disappointing, anticlimactic, or simply don't match your expectations. These approaches have been helpful for many people who take psychedelics for recreation and have also been employed in research studies, so they are tried and true.

We suggest you begin with **setting an intention**—which is not the same as a goal. Setting an intention is about forming meaningful hopes or purposes that you carry into the experience. It's a guiding principle that can help you navigate the vast and sometimes unpredictable landscape of the psychedelic state. Research has shown that setting intentions can have a significant impact on your experience (Healy, Lee, and D'Andrea 2021). For example, one study (Haijen et al. 2018) found that individuals who set intentions were more likely to report mystical experiences and report fewer challenging moments while using classic psychedelics. Similarly, another study (Elmer et al. 2024) found that those who added "intentions focused on gaining insights" experienced more positive social-emotional outcomes, such as increased empathy and improved relationships, compared to those who focused solely on hedonistic intentions (like seeking euphoria or energy).

Those who set meaningful intentions may find it easier to let go and allow the session to flow without resistance, opening themselves to receive the benefits and navigate any challenges that may arise. In psychedelic therapy, clients are often encouraged to include letting go as part of their intention for the session (Wolff et al. 2020). We invite you to embrace this practice of intention setting as you prepare for your experience. We also suggest bringing an attitude of openness and curiosity toward the experience. A nonjudgmental awareness can be immensely helpful. By fostering an attitude of openness and curiosity, you enhance your psychological resilience, making it easier to remain flexible yet stable in the face of the unknown (Campo and Yali 2024).

Next, let's talk about **being vs. doing** while on psychedelics. Most current models of psychedelic therapy or treatment with classic psychedelics recommend that patients do not engage in complex tasks or exercises during the acute effects of a psychedelic. Conversation should be limited to supportive comments and actions from the therapist or facilitator to promote safety and provide reassurance. The participants do not engage in psychotherapy during the session. This is a change from early psychedelic therapy models where the therapist would intentionally try to create a specific type of experience for the client. Some **underground practitioners** still use the older model. If you are going to work with a guide, facilitator, or therapist—either in a clinical or research setting or an underground therapy setting—it is important to understand beforehand how much they will engage with you.

Although we encourage curiosity and openness, and we emphasize being vs. doing, sometimes those who are familiar with psychedelic states want to engage in a specific project or task, such as an art project, creative movement choreography, or a journaling exercise. This can be a valid choice depending on your intentions or goals. Perhaps you hope to foster creative expression or translate your experience into something enduring that others can interact with. We caution you to hold any such plans lightly, enjoy them if they should seem like the right thing at the time, and let them go if other needs arise in the moment.

While setting intentions and cultivating an attitude of openness are vital for a meaningful psychedelic experience, it's equally important to be mindful of factors that might lead to challenging or difficult moments during your journey. One significant factor is entering the experience with a mind preoccupied by day-to-day concerns. Being mentally entangled in everyday worries can contribute to feelings of dread or anxiety once the psychedelic effects begin (Russ et al. 2019). Research has indicated that individuals who start their session in a state of preoccupation have more challenging experiences (Metzner, Litwin, and Weil 1965). This is consistent with the finding that **neuroticism** is associated with challenging experiences with psilocybin (Barrett, Johnson, and Griffiths 2017). The result can be feelings of powerlessness or fear during the experience—often referred to as a **bad trip** (Barrett et al. 2016).

We recommend that you make a conscious effort to not only set aside daily concerns before your session, but also engage in mindfulness practices, such as meditation or deep breathing, prior to and during your journey. By relinquishing your preoccupations, you allow yourself to fully immerse in the present moment, reducing the likelihood of difficult emotions.

Even with optimal preparation, it's still possible for feelings of fear and confusion to arise unexpectedly. These emotions are common in many psychedelic experiences (Johnstad 2021). When these feelings come up, they can be disorienting, even overwhelming. However, there are ways to navigate through these moments that can transform a potentially distressing situation into a valuable opportunity for insight and growth (Carbonaro et al. 2016).

Fear, particularly the fear of **ego dissolution** or of losing control, can occur during a challenging psychedelic journey (Johnstad 2021). In these moments, it can be helpful to remember that fear is a natural reaction to an unusual and unfamiliar state of consciousness. It's understandable and normal to feel afraid. As we keep saying, openness and curiosity will help. Don't resist or fight this fear. Acknowledging the emotion and allowing it to move through you can help the fear to dissipate. Often, individuals find that once the initial wave of fear passes, they enter into profound feelings of peace and unity.

Confusion often accompanies fear during psychedelic experiences (Johnstad 2021). The mind may feel overwhelmed by the rapid succession of thoughts, images, or emotions, leading to a sense of chaos. In these moments, grounding techniques such as focusing on the breath can be incredibly helpful. Slow, deep breathing can calm the nervous system, allowing you to regain a sense of presence amidst the confusion. By anchoring your awareness in the present moment, you create space for the experience to unfold naturally, without being swept away by the flood of thoughts or sensations. As with fear, confusion often arises from the mind's attempt to grasp and control the psychedelic experience. Letting go of the need to understand everything immediately can help ease the confusion, transforming it into a space for unexpected insights to emerge.

No matter what uncomfortable feelings arise, it can be helpful—especially with therapeutic support—to stay with the discomfort rather than trying to escape it. This is why we emphasize the importance of curiosity. Approaching these sensations with an open mind can lead to greater understanding and healing. However, there are clear situations where your discomfort may signal something more than an internal challenge. If a facilitator engages in unethical or inappropriate behavior, curiosity and openness are not enough. In these instances, it is crucial to trust your instincts. It's always appropriate to set boundaries or revoke consent if something feels wrong. Your well-being must remain the top priority.

Fear and confusion, while uncomfortable, are natural parts of the psychedelic experience and can be navigated with openness, patience, and trust. Think of these emotions as part of the healing and transformative process that psychedelics offer. By meeting them with curiosity rather than resistance, you can allow yourself to explore deeper levels of understanding and personal growth.

The key to navigating challenging experiences is to remain flexible yet stable in the face of the unknown. This openness not only enriches your journey but also empowers you to integrate difficult experiences in meaningful ways. With self-compassion and awareness, even the most challenging moments can lead to profound insights.

## Setting Intentions and Letting Go

Intentions can serve as helpful guideposts during a psychedelic experience. However, it's also important to hold these intentions lightly and allow your experience to unfold on its own.

**Objective:** Set intentions while cultivating an open, accepting mindset.

**Instructions:**

1. Find a quiet, comfortable place where you can reflect without interruption. Take a few slow, deep breaths to relax and center yourself in the present moment.

2. Reflect on what feels most important to you at this time in your life. What challenges are you facing? In what areas do you hope to grow, heal, or gain insight? Jot down a few key themes that emerge.

3. Now, for each theme, create a simple intention starting with "May I..." Some examples may include:

   "May I open to new perspectives."

"May I practice self-compassion."

"May I release that which no longer serves me."

"May I connect with my inner wisdom."

4.  Read through your intentions, noticing how well they resonate with you. You are free to adjust the wording until each one feels right to you. Aim for two concise intentions.

5.  Now imagine holding these intentions in open hands, palms facing upward. Picture yourself carrying them with a light, relaxed grip—holding them gently and lightly.

6.  Acknowledge that once you take the psychedelic medicine, the journey will unfold as it will, in ways you may not expect. Affirm to yourself: "I hold these intentions lightly. I release attachment to any particular outcome. I am open to whatever wisdom and healing this experience brings."

7.  Record your intentions where you can refer back to them later. But remember, once the journey begins, allow your intentions to drift into the background as you surrender to the experience. Know that you may connect with them in direct or indirect ways.

By setting mindful intentions and consciously holding them with lightness, you plant seeds to enrich your journey while making space for unexpected insights and experiences to emerge. Intentions are meant to be your helpful guides, not rigid goals to fixate upon.

## Cultivating Openness and Curiosity

**Objective:** To develop an attitude of openness and curiosity toward one's inner experiences, in preparation for navigating the unique states of consciousness that may arise during a psychedelic journey. The mantra you develop here can stay with you throughout your journey.

**Instructions:**

1.  Take a comfortable seated position in a quiet place where you won't be disturbed. Close your eyes and take a few deep, slow breaths, allowing your body to settle and your mind to arrive in the present moment.

2.  Imagine you are about to embark on a journey to a place you've never been before. It could be a foreign country, a natural wonder, or even a fantastical realm. Visualize yourself standing at the threshold of this new territory that is filled with unknown landscapes, experiences, and encounters.

3.  As you contemplate crossing this threshold, notice any feelings of excitement, nervousness, or uncertainty that arise. Acknowledge these feelings without judgment, and then gently redirect your attention to a sense of pure curiosity and wonder.

4.  Now, create a personal mantra or affirmation that captures your intention to approach this journey with openness and curiosity. Your mantra should be short, positive, and easy to remember. Some examples might include:

    "I open to the unknown with curiosity and wonder."

    "Each moment is an opportunity for discovery."

    "I trust in the wisdom of my journey."

5.  Take a moment to repeat your chosen mantra several times, either silently or out loud. Notice how it feels to embody this attitude of openness and curiosity.

6.  Now, imagine taking your first steps into this new world. As you encounter unfamiliar sights, sounds, sensations, and experiences, practice greeting each one with an open and curious mind. Whenever you notice yourself feeling overwhelmed, confused, or resistant, silently repeat your mantra to yourself as a reminder to stay open and curious.

7.  Continue on this imaginary journey, using your mantra as an anchor to maintain an attitude of open-minded exploration. Embrace the novelty and uncertainty of each moment. Let go of the need to control or understand.

8.  When you feel ready, take a few deep breaths and slowly open your eyes. Allow yourself to return to the present moment.

9.  Reflect on your experience. How did it feel to use your personal mantra as a reminder to stay open and curious? Did it help you to navigate challenges or uncertainty? Write down your observations and any insights you gained.

    _____

    _____

    _____

    _____

    _____

    _____

10. Practice this visualization exercise regularly, using your personal mantra each time. As you become more comfortable with this practice, start to bring your mantra and the attitude it represents into your daily life and your anticipated psychedelic journey.

As you prepare for your psychedelic experience, remember your mantra and the intention it represents. If you find yourself feeling anxious, overwhelmed, or closed off during your journey, silently repeat your mantra to yourself as a reminder to reopen to the experience with curiosity and wonder.

The best way to handle a challenging psychedelic experience is to relinquish any attempt to control or change what is occurring. Simply allowing the sensations to be felt will enable you to move through the experience. We call this the concept of **in and through**.

However, it may not always be possible for you to go in and through. So we encourage you to create what we call a toolbox. Your toolbox is a list of actions you may take if you find yourself in an overwhelming or distressing psychedelic experience.

## Toolbox for Navigating a Difficult Experience

**Objective:** To create a personalized list of actions and techniques that can be used to navigate challenging or overwhelming moments during a psychedelic experience.

**Instructions:**

1. Write down specific actions that may help you when you are feeling distressed. Write down as many as you can think of. Some examples might include:

   o   Breathing deeply and slowly

   o   Focusing on sensations in the body

   o   Repeating a comforting mantra or phrase

   o   Visualizing a safe, peaceful place

   o   Reaching out for support from a trusted friend or therapist

   o   Engaging in a grounding activity like drawing or stretching

   o   Reminding yourself that the experience is temporary and will pass

   o   Changing your physical position or environment (for example, sitting up or moving to a different room)

   o   Listening to soothing music or sounds

     o    Engaging with a comforting object like a soft blanket or meaningful photograph

     o    Expressing your emotions through movement, sound, or writing

     o    Asking your facilitator for support or reassurance

2. Review your list and star or highlight 5–10 techniques that feel best to you. These will form the core of your toolbox.

3. For each of your core techniques, write a brief script or set of instructions for yourself on how to use this tool. Be as specific as possible. For example: "Take 10 slow, deep breaths. Inhale for a count of 4, hold for 4, exhale for 6. Focus all of your attention on the sensations of the breath moving in and out of your body."

4. Create a concise, easily readable sheet of your core toolbox techniques. This could be a physical document that you can keep with you, or a digital file that you can access on your phone. Include the name of each technique, your specific instructions, and any helpful reminders or affirmations (for example, "This too shall pass," "I am safe," "I have the resources to handle this").

_____

_____

_____

_____

_____

_____

5. Share your toolbox with your facilitator or therapist. Ask for their feedback and any additional suggestions they might have. Incorporate their input as feels appropriate.

6. Prior to your psychedelic session, review your toolbox sheet.

Remember, while it's impossible to predict or control every aspect of your psychedelic journey, having a toolbox of coping techniques can significantly increase your confidence and capacity to navigate challenging experiences. Trust that you have the inner resources and outer support to handle whatever arises. With preparation, self-compassion, and a spirit of open curiosity, challenges can become valuable opportunities for growth and self-discovery.

Sometimes, it can feel like nothing much happened during a psychedelic experience. This can be disappointing or upsetting. But there are ways to find value even in such experiences.

# Working with Underwhelming Experiences

**Objective:** To help you work with a psychedelic experience that was underwhelming—where it seemed like nothing out of the ordinary happened.

**Instructions:**

1. Recall the psychedelic experience in which you felt that nothing happened. Write down a brief description of your intentions going into the experience.

   _____

   _____

   _____

   _____

2. Reflect on the following questions and write down your responses:

   o  What were your expectations or hopes going into the experience? How might these have influenced your perception of the journey?

   o  Were there any moments of heightened sensation, emotion, or awareness, even if fleeting? What were these like?

   o  Were there any periods of challenge, discomfort, or difficulty? How did you navigate these?

   o  What was your overall state of mind during the experience? Were you anxious, relaxed, curious, bored? How might this have affected your experience?

   o  How did you feel in the days following the experience? Any changes in mood, perspective, or behavior, even subtle ones?

   _____

   _____

   _____

   _____

   _____

   _____

3.  Now, imagine you are discussing your experience with a wise, compassionate friend. This friend says to you, "In the realm of inner exploration, every moment of consciousness is a happening—a unique, unrepeatable event in the unfolding of your awareness. Even if the content of the experience did not meet your expectations, the process of journeying inward is inherently valuable. It takes courage, curiosity, and openness to venture into the unknown landscape of your own mind. That, in itself, is significant."

4.  Sit with this perspective for a few minutes, letting it sink in. Does it resonate with you? How does it shift your perspective on your experience, if at all? Write down your reflections.

5.  Now, revisit your description of the psychedelic experience from step 1. Reread it through the lens of this new perspective. Look for moments or aspects of the journey that may hold deeper significance than you initially thought. Consider:

    o   Were there any challenges or discomforts you handled with presence and resilience?

    o   Did you have any insights, however small, that could be seeds for further growth and exploration?

    o   Did the very act of turning inward and dedicating time to self-exploration feel meaningful or nourishing in some way?

    o   Even if the journey felt uneventful, did it give you any clarity on your intentions or areas for future growth?

6.  Write a revised reflection on your psychedelic experience, one that honors the inherent value in the process of inner exploration, regardless of the content or outcomes. Acknowledge your own courage, curiosity, and commitment to growth.

7.  As you continue to integrate your psychedelic experience, return to this practice of looking for meaning in the seemingly insignificant. Remember, every moment of turning toward your inner world with openness and nonjudgment plants seeds that can blossom in unexpected ways over time.

By reframing the underwhelming experience, you are opening to the possibility that every inner journey, even an uneventful one, holds inherent meaning and value. You are developing the capacity to glean wisdom and insight from the full spectrum of your psychedelic experiences. This shift in perspective can significantly deepen and enrich your overall journey with psychedelics and your own unfolding path of growth and self-discovery.

In principle, every type of psychedelic experience offers opportunities for value if you meet it with openness and curiosity. Set your intentions but hold them loosely and let the experience evolve as it will. Even an experience in which it seems nothing happened can provide you with a chance to learn about yourself. The exercises in this chapter will help you to prepare for or cope with any type of experience. If you are faced with a challenging or difficult experience, remember that it is best not to try to change or control it. Just let yourself feel the sensations and move in and through the experience. If this proves to be impossible, the toolbox of resources and techniques that you prepared using the exercise above will help you get through any difficult sensations. Your inner journey may not unfold as you expect or even as you wish, but the tools you develop here will help you navigate the sensations and glean from them the insights that will help you to grow and make the healthy changes you seek.

The next three chapters focus on the integration of the psychedelic experience, during the time immediately post-experience, the days and weeks afterward, and in the longer term—including lifelong shifts you may make. Integration is widely discussed in the field of psychedelic research. Research studies usually include at least two integration or follow-up sessions, sometimes more. But integration really takes place outside of the therapy session, in real life where the impacts of the psychedelic experience are felt. While there isn't a standard model for integration, there are some best practices, established ways of working with difficulties, and resources you can turn to for support.

# CHAPTER 6

# Coming Home

This chapter focuses on the first hours and days after your psychedelic experience—the time when you return home, unpack your bags, do the laundry, check the mail, and reorient yourself to daily life, all while reflecting on the journey you've just undertaken. As the experience ends, the intensity subsides, and you begin to reconnect with your surroundings. As the more intense alterations in your visual, auditory, sensory, and emotional landscapes fade away, subtle shifts in your understanding and way of relating to the world may emerge. Even after the immediate effects have worn off, it might take a good night's sleep or two to fully arrive back in your usual state of awareness.

In the hours and days following your psychedelic experience, you might notice a range of feelings and thoughts emerging. You could feel a profound sense of peace, with an improved mood and reduced anxiety (Nygart et al. 2022). Alternatively, you might experience confusion, emotional reactivity, or feelings of vulnerability (Johnstad 2021). Understanding that these responses are normal can help you navigate this period with greater ease and prepare you for the longer integration process. Depending on the psychedelic you chose, the nature of your journey, and your individual circumstances, these changes can vary widely. You may want to hold onto the intensity and delight you felt during the peak moments. Or you may worry about forgetting the insights you gained. Although you want to do the best you can to retain what was helpful for you, it's not possible nor desirable to be in a psychedelic state all the time. Remember that what is most important from your journey will not be lost. Even if the feelings aren't as vivid later on, it's something that you have experienced and you may find yourself reconnecting to over time.

Making sense of profound experiences, in the hours and days after a psychedelic journey, can feel overwhelming. You might struggle to reconcile new insights with your previous beliefs or find it challenging to incorporate this awareness into your daily routine (Lutkajtis and Evans 2023). Difficulties in adapting back to everyday life can create feelings of disconnection, frustration, or anxiety (Cowley-Court et al. 2023). Recognizing these challenges is the first step toward weaving your experiences into the fabric of your life. How you understand and put these feelings into context can impact their effect on you (McMillan 2021). It can be tempting to draw conclusions about who you've become, believe that you will be like this forever, or become preoccupied with how you need to change after a psychedelic experience. Patience and self-compassion can be helpful during the change process (Agin-Liebes et al. 2023). Give yourself permission to take the time you need to process and integrate your journey.

Taking care of your body is crucial during the period immediately after a psychedelic experience. Simple acts like nourishing yourself with healthy food, getting adequate sleep, and engaging in regular physical activity can stabilize your mood and energy levels. Activities that promote relaxation and grounding—such as gentle yoga, mindful walking, or deep breathing exercises—can enhance your physical and mental resilience (Holas and Kamińska 2023). By tending to your body's needs, you create a solid foundation for your mind to process and integrate new experiences effectively.

Finding meaning in your experience is a vital part of integration (Amada and Shane 2022; Hartogsohn 2018). Take some time to reflect on the insights you've gained and consider how they relate to your life.

Journaling can be especially helpful, allowing you to express thoughts and emotions and clarify your insights. By actively engaging with your thoughts and feelings, you'll begin to see how your journey can fit into your everyday world.

Meaning and integration isn't only achieved using words or language. Creative expression through art, music, or other nonverbal activity can provide powerful avenues for exploration (Koretz 2022). All of this is useful in the period immediately after a psychedelic journey. However, recognize that there is time to make meaning and that your process may shift and change in the upcoming weeks and months.

Discussing your experiences with a trusted, open-minded friend or family member who can listen without judgment may also aid in this process. Connecting with others who have undergone similar experiences can be incredibly helpful as well (Cowley-Court et al. 2023; Skiles et al. 2023). Support groups, integration circles, and helplines offer containers to share stories, gain insights, and receive encouragement (Pleet et al. 2023). Building a community around you can ease feelings of isolation and promote collective healing. Such communities may even be as important as the psychedelic experience itself (Gezon 2024)! This being said, it's crucial to remember that peers may not provide the same kind of legal and ethical safety (such as confidentiality) that a professional will. Also, peers may not be equipped to support some of the more intense symptoms or struggles you may have.

While many move through the integration phase smoothly, some may encounter challenges that require professional support. If you experience persistent emotional distress, difficulty functioning in daily life, or a worsening of preexisting mental health conditions, it might be time to seek help from a mental health professional with experience in psychedelics (Greń et al. 2023b). Recognizing when to reach out is crucial for ensuring your safety and well-being. Professional guidance can provide additional resources and strategies to support you during this time. If you have preexisting mental health conditions, it's especially important to approach integration with additional support. Tailored strategies and professional guidance can help manage symptoms and minimize adverse effects.

There is no one-size-fits-all prescription for this period of time. Your experience and how you integrate it can depend on many factors, such as the setting of your journey—be it therapeutic, ceremonial, or recreational. Your cultural background and personal beliefs also play a significant role (Dupuis 2022; Hartogsohn 2020). In the hours and days immediately following your psychedelic experience, be open to the range of emotions and thoughts that surface, which can be a normal part of the integration process. By practicing patience and self-compassion, taking care of your physical well-being, and engaging in activities that help you find meaning—whether through journaling, creative expression, or connecting with others—you can begin to weave the insights from your journey into the fabric of your daily life. Again, if challenges arise during this critical initial period, don't hesitate to seek professional support to ensure your well-being. Trust that with time, openness, and care, you'll integrate your experiences in a way that honors your journey and supports your continued growth.

# Identifying the Need for Social Support and Professional Help After a Psychedelic Experience

After a psychedelic experience, it's a good idea to have a support system that can help you process and integrate your experience. Feeling heard and validated can help increase a sense of connectedness and safety. Therapy or coaching can be helpful when a provider is educated about psychedelic experiences.

You may wonder how to know when you need support from trusted friends or family members and when it's necessary to seek professional help from a doctor or psychotherapist. In our experience, it's important to reach out to a trusted person when you:

- Feel overwhelmed by emotions or thoughts related to your psychedelic experience

- Have difficulty processing or making sense of your experience

- Feel isolated or disconnected from others

- Need a safe space to share your experience without fear of judgment

- Want guidance on integrating insights or lessons learned during your experience into your daily life

Here are the qualities to look for when choosing a trusted person:

- Someone who is open-minded and nonjudgmental about psychedelic experiences

- A person who is a good listener and emotionally supportive

- Someone who has personal experience with psychedelics or is knowledgeable about their effects

- A person whom you trust to maintain confidentiality about your experience

When reaching out for social support, remember these guidelines:

1. Choose a time and place where you feel comfortable and safe to discuss your experience.

2. Be honest about your feelings and any challenges you're facing after the experience.

3. Be open to feedback and advice, but remember that your experience is unique to you.

4. Express gratitude for their support and understanding.

# Identifying the Need for Professional Help

While social support is crucial, there are times when seeking professional help from a doctor or psychotherapist is necessary. Consider reaching out for professional help if you:

- Experience prolonged or severe symptoms of anxiety, depression, or other mental health issues following your psychedelic experience

- Have difficulty functioning in your daily life (work, school, relationships) due to the impact of your experience

- Experience persistent flashbacks or visual disturbances that cause distress or impair functioning

- Have thoughts of self-harm or suicide

- Find yourself doing more risk-taking behaviors or substance abuse following your experience

- Have a preexisting mental health condition that has worsened after your psychedelic experience

- Feel that your experience has triggered past traumas and unresolved emotional issues that require professional support

When seeking professional help:

- Look for a mental health professional who has experience working with clients who have used psychedelics or has knowledge about psychedelic-assisted therapy

- Be honest about your psychedelic use and any symptoms or challenges you're experiencing

- If you have a preexisting mental health condition, inform your provider about your psychedelic experience and any changes in symptoms

- Follow your provider's recommendations for treatment, which may include therapy, medication, or both

- Look for a therapist who will help you develop your own understanding without imposing too much of their own worldview

Remember, seeking help is a sign of strength, not weakness. By reaching out for support when needed, you are taking an active role in your own healing and growth process.

# CHAPTER 7

# Settling In

It's important to acknowledge that research on the long-term aspects of psychedelic integration is still in its early stages. We've personally made contributions to the theory of integration drawing from evidence-based practices (Gorman et al. 2021) In this chapter, we share some of the insights we've gained from our hands-on experience with integration. But there is still a significant need for further research to deepen our evolving understanding of this complex process (Greń et al. 2023a).

It has been said that a psychedelic experience is like 10 years of psychotherapy in one night. It's also been said that such an experience is like 10 years of insight in one night. But insight is not the same as change. The purpose of this chapter is to support you through the integration process, helping you turn psychedelic-inspired shifts into tangible steps toward personal growth.

We will explore experiences common to the integration phase, including the honeymoon period of post-psychedelic optimism, which can sometimes lead to unrealistic expectations. We'll also delve into some of the challenges that can arise, such as feelings of disappointment if the journey didn't meet your expectations. These emotions are natural and, as discussed in the prior chapter, can be a part of the integration process. You'll also learn how to navigate the ups and downs of this nonlinear journey, how to work through discomfort, and how to recognize that real change often occurs in subtle, incremental ways.

Finally, we'll explore the unfolding process, where growth and healing can emerge spontaneously over time, and how values-based actions and behavioral activation can help maintain the positive changes you experience. Through the exercises provided, this chapter will support you in staying open to this ongoing journey, helping you align your daily actions with your core values, and encouraging sustainable personal development.

# The Psychedelic Honeymoon

In the weeks following your psychedelic journey, you might find yourself in what is often referred to as the "honeymoon" phase. During this time, it's possible to feel a heightened sense of optimism, believing that the psychedelic experience holds the answers to all your challenges. You may idealize the psychedelic itself and the insights gained, viewing them as universally positive and without drawbacks (Guss 2022). This period can be both exhilarating and inspiring, filling you with enthusiasm and a renewed zest for life.

However, as the honeymoon phase begins to wane, you might start to recognize that integrating these profound experiences into your everyday life requires ongoing effort and patience. The initial excitement may give way to the realization that psychedelics are not a cure-all; they are tools that can catalyze change but cannot do the work for you. Acknowledging the limitations of psychedelics allows you to engage more authentically with the integration process. This involves facing challenges, addressing areas that psychedelics may not have resolved, and committing to the sometimes demanding work of transforming insights into lasting change. Embracing this reality can lead to deeper personal growth and a more balanced relationship with the psychedelic experience.

# Working with Disappointment

During the integration phase after a psychedelic experience, you might find yourself grappling with feelings of disappointment. Perhaps you didn't encounter the insights or transformative moments you had anticipated. Understanding that these feelings of disappointment are normal can help you navigate this period with greater ease and support your ongoing integration process. It's common to set specific intentions or hold high expectations about what you hope to achieve, and when reality doesn't align with these hopes, it's natural to feel let down. Accepting these emotions without judgment can allow you to process them (Campo 2022).

Your expectations can significantly shape how you perceive your experience, which is why we discuss mindset, motivation, and intention setting in previous chapters (Colloca, Nikayin, and Sanacora 2023). Even if it seems like nothing happened during and after your psychedelic experience, subtle shifts may have occurred beneath the surface. Growth can manifest in small, incremental ways as well as in more dramatic forms. Pay attention to minor changes in your thoughts, feelings, or behaviors—you might notice a slight increase in patience, a new perspective on a familiar challenge, or a subtle change in how you relate to others. These small shifts are meaningful steps on your path to self-discovery.

Working through disappointment involves letting go of the need to control outcomes. Remember, psychedelic experiences are inherently unpredictable, and surrendering to the process can be a powerful lesson in itself. Embracing uncertainty allows you to be present with whatever arises, opening doors to insights that rigid expectations might have obscured. Be gentle with yourself and acknowledge the courage it took to embark on your journey in the first place. That courage alone can be an experience to work with and build on.

What might initially seem like an **underwhelming experience** can offer valuable lessons. For example, the quietness of the journey may have highlighted your expectations or revealed your discomfort with stillness. Viewing the experience through this lens can transform disappointment into an opportunity for learning and self-awareness. And if you still find yourself feeling like nothing happened, that's okay too. Some challenges require ongoing effort, additional support, or different approaches altogether. As you'll see as you read on, change can be a nonlinear process, full of unexpected twists and turns. By remaining open, you allow for opportunities for change to emerge over time. How you understand and frame these feelings can significantly impact their effect on you. Give yourself permission to take the time you need to process and integrate what happened.

# Revisiting Nonlinear Change and the Unfolding Process

During the integration phase, it's essential to recognize that change may not always follow a predictable path. In earlier chapters, we introduced the concept of nonlinear change—shifts that can happen rapidly, unexpectedly, and sometimes feel unsettling (Hipólito et al. 2023). We also explored the unfolding process, a metaphor that speaks to the spontaneous emergence of personal or spiritual growth when someone deeply engages with their inner world (Welwood 1982). Both concepts—nonlinear change and the unfolding process—are central to understanding the integration period, which can extend weeks or even months after a psychedelic journey.

It's common to assume that progress always feels positive, but nonlinear change and the unfolding process can be challenging and uncomfortable. To illustrate this: imagine a woman who uses psychedelics to process the trauma of childhood physical abuse. As a coping mechanism, she had internalized the belief that she deserved the harm she experienced. After preparing for her journey and undergoing a powerful psychedelic session, she begins to feel less burdened by her traumatic memories. But then a new awareness emerges. She realizes she never deserved the abuse, and this brings up intense anger toward those who hurt her. While this anger is a sign of her growing self-worth, it also creates discomfort. She struggles with this new emotion, sometimes feeling irritable with people in her current life who had no part in her past trauma. And in her culture, irritability expressed by a woman is dismissed and ignored.

In this case, her anger is part of the healing process, a sign of the shifts in her trauma recovery. However, it's easy for someone in a similar position to wonder if these difficult emotions are simply a side effect of the psychedelic itself, especially from a purely biological perspective. And indeed, sometimes emotions can be linked to neurobiological changes brought on by the psychedelic. This is where adopting a holistic biopsychosocial approach can be helpful—it allows space for the biological, psychological, and cultural aspects of integration (Gorman et al. 2021).

During this time, cultivating discernment becomes key. This means taking the time to reflect on your emotions, even the uncomfortable ones. Instead of pushing them away, sit with them, explore their origins, and consider how they might connect to your personal history or your recent psychedelic experience. Ask yourself: Can these feelings offer something useful? How might they inform how I move through the world now? This self-reflection is part of the integration process.

If the emotions you're experiencing feel overwhelming, unhelpful, or disconnected from anything meaningful in your life, it's important to reach out for support. A mental health professional experienced in psychedelics can help you navigate these complexities and guide you through the integration process.

# Values-Based Actions and Behavioral Activation

As you read this chapter, you might wonder how to maintain the benefits you've experienced thus far. A psychedelic study participant once asked, "How can I keep these positive changes long after my session?" The therapist replied, "Any way you can." While this answer might seem vague at first, it holds a valuable truth. There are many methods you may find useful, such as meditation, yoga, or journaling.

However, these practices are often generalized approaches and may not fully address the unique needs or struggles of each person. In this workbook, we aim to go beyond that. We encourage you to notice shifts in your own beliefs and values. By aligning your actions with your personal values (Hayes and Pierson 2005), you can find a way to maintain and integrate the changes that most resonate with you. This approach can be built on through behavioral activation, which means taking small action steps that build into a **positive feedback loop**, supporting new ways of feeling and being in the world (Kanter et al. 2010).

These are not the only pathways to integration (Bathje, Majeski, and Kudowor 2022). Some find meaningful change through spiritual practices, periods of rest and inaction, or unconscious shifts or biological change through the pharmacological effects of psychedelics. We have chosen to highlight activities that emphasize positive reinforcement through behavioral action. You will find such exercise below, designed to support you in integrating your experience in a way that aligns with some of the shifts you may have experienced.

# Bringing It All Together

A psychedelic experience can be a powerful catalyst for insight and change, but sustainable change comes through how you integrate these insights into your daily life. While the initial honeymoon phase following a journey can be filled with optimism and enthusiasm, the deeper work lies in maintaining balance and commitment as you face the challenges that can follow. Disappointments, nonlinear progress, and emotional upheaval are all part of the process. These experiences are opportunities for self-reflection, growth, and learning.

As you engage in this unfolding process, remember that change may not happen all at once or in the ways you expect. Small, incremental shifts in thoughts, behaviors, or perspectives can be just as valuable as dramatic realizations. Your journey will require patience, self-compassion, and, at times, the support of others. The exercises in this chapter are designed to help you reflect on these subtle shifts, address difficult emotions, and align your actions with your core values. By taking these intentional steps, you can cultivate lasting change and sustain the benefits of your psychedelic experience over time. Remember, integration is a continuous, evolving process. Revisiting these practices and reflecting on your journey regularly will keep you connected to your growth and personal development.

# Exercise 1: Post-Experience Reflection and Coping Exercise

This exercise is designed to help you reflect on a difficult psychedelic experience. It will help you identify the challenges you encountered and find support.

**Describe your experience.** Write a brief description of your challenging psychedelic experience. What happened during the experience itself? What kinds of difficulties did you experience afterward, and for how long?

_____

_____

_____

_____

**Identify difficulties.** Review the list of difficulties below reported by people who've had challenging psychedelic experiences. Check all that apply to your situation.

- ☐ Emotional (anxiety, depression, mood swings, etc.)

- ☐ Perceptual (visual distortions, flashbacks, hallucinations)

- ☐ Cognitive (confused thinking, rumination, memory issues)

- ☐ Sense of self (depersonalization, loss of identity/**agency**)

- ☐ Social (disconnection, withdrawal, **interpersonal sensitivity**)

- ☐ Somatic (sleep issues, appetite changes, unusual body sensations)

- ☐ Existential/spiritual (loss of meaning, fear of insanity/death, metaphysical confusion)

- ☐ Other types of difficulties you may have experienced:

_____

_____

**Assess risk factors.** What factors may have increased the risks for you? These could include high doses, lack of preparation/guidance, prior trauma or mental health issues, a combination of substances, or other factors. Write down the risk factors that applied to your situation.

_____

_____

_____

**Consider immediate support.** Reflect on the difficulties and risk factors you identified. Do you need immediate support from a professional, or do you feel safe and capable of continuing your integration on your own? If you need immediate support, please contact a professional. You may wish to refer to the section "Identifying the Need for Social Support and Professional Help After a Psychedelic Experience" in the previous chapter.

**Reflect on positive changes.** Despite the difficulties, have you noticed any positive changes since the experience? Are there any lessons or insights you can draw from this experience? Write down any that come to mind.

_____

_____

_____

_____

Now write down any inner strengths or outer support systems that are helping you cope and heal.

_____

_____

_____

_____

Coping methods for integration include confiding in caring others, journaling, meditation/relaxation techniques, focusing on self-care, and seeking professional support if needed. What coping methods have you tried, and what else could you experiment with? List 3–5 constructive coping practices you can use going forward.

_____

_____

_____

_____

_____

_____

Remember, integration is a process that unfolds over time. Be patient and compassionate with yourself. With commitment to self-care and support, even the most difficult psychedelic experiences can, in time, become sources of insight, empowerment, and positive transformation.

The unfolding process refers to the natural, organic development of one's inner self and personal growth. After a psychedelic experience, this process can be particularly profound, revealing layers of insight and transformation. The next personal reflection exercise is designed to help you explore and integrate these revelations, fostering deeper understanding and growth.

# Exercise 2: Exploring the Unfolding Process

**Instructions:**

**Set the scene.** Find a quiet, comfortable space where you can reflect without interruptions. Gather this workbook (or a journal or notebook), a pen, and any other items that help you feel relaxed and centered, such as candles, soothing music, or a cozy blanket.

**Ground yourself.** Begin with a few minutes of deep breathing or meditation to center yourself. Close your eyes, take several slow, deep breaths, and allow your body and mind to relax. Focus on being present in the moment.

**Reflect on your experience.** Write a brief summary of your recent psychedelic experience. Include details about what happened, significant moments, emotions you felt, and any key insights or realizations.

_____

_____

_____

_____

_____

_____

**Identify key themes.** Look over your summary and identify 2–3 key themes or insights that emerged during your experience. These could be related to your personal growth, relationships, spiritual beliefs, or any other aspect of your life.

**Deepen your exploration.** For each key theme or insight, reflect on the following questions and write your responses:

- What was the most profound realization or feeling associated with this theme?

- How does this insight relate to your current life situation or personal challenges?

- What emotions or memories does this insight evoke?

- How has this insight changed your perspective or understanding of yourself and the world?

_____

_____

_____

_____

_____

**Envision the unfolding process**. Imagine how these insights might unfold in your life moving forward. Reflect on the following questions:

- What steps can you take to integrate these insights into your daily life?

- How can you nurture and support this unfolding process?

- What changes or actions do you feel inspired to pursue as a result of these insights?

- How can you stay mindful and present to continue growing and evolving?

_____

_____

_____

_____

**Commit to your growth**. Write down two or three specific actions or practices you can commit to in the coming weeks to support your unfolding process. These might include setting aside time for regular reflection, seeking support from a therapist or mentor, engaging in creative expression, or making lifestyle changes that align with your new insights.

_____

_____

_____

_____

**Closing reflection**. End your exercise with a brief meditation or moment of silence. Close your eyes, take a few deep breaths, and silently express gratitude for the insights you have gained and the journey of unfolding that lies ahead.

As part of preparation, we asked you to reflect on the values and beliefs you hold as you consider whether to have a psychedelic experience. The next exercise aims to help you identify and understand any changes or affirmations in your beliefs, values, and sense of self following your psychedelic journey.

## Exercise 3: Exploring Shifts in Values and Beliefs After Your Psychedelic Experience

Locate the exercise in Chapter 2 where you listed your core beliefs and values. Take some time to read through your responses thoughtfully. After reviewing your initial reflections, we invite you to notice how you feel about each item now.

For each category, write down any new thoughts, feelings, or perspectives that have emerged.

- Have any of your core beliefs about yourself, others, or the world changed?

- Are there beliefs that have been strengthened or challenged?

- Do you feel more deeply committed to certain values, or have new guiding principles emerged? Are there values that no longer resonate with you as strongly?

- Has your interpretation of past significant events changed?

- Have new insights or lessons surfaced from reflecting on these experiences?

_____

_____

_____

_____

_____

_____

_____

Create a side-by-side comparison for each category, noting the differences and similarities between your before and after reflections. Highlight any areas where significant shifts have occurred.

For each change you've noted, consider the following questions:

- What do these changes mean to you?

- How might they influence your future actions and decisions?

- Are there any feelings of excitement, apprehension, or curiosity associated with these changes?

Identify specific ways you can incorporate these new insights or affirmed beliefs into your daily life. Set one or two realistic intentions or goals that align with your current values and beliefs.

_____

_____

_____

_____

_____

The next exercise aims to help you identify specific actions that reflect your current beliefs and values after your psychedelic experience, empowering you to incorporate these actions into your daily life.

## Exercise 4: Turning Values into Action

**Reconnect with your core values.** Look back at the values and beliefs you identified in the previous exercise or take a moment to consider what feels most important to you now. Write down three values that resonate most strongly with you at this time. Examples might include compassion, creativity, authenticity, environmental stewardship, or community.

_____

_____

_____

_____

**Define value-based activities**. For each value you named above, list activities that embody or express that value in real life. For example:

- *Compassion:* Volunteering at a local shelter

- *Creativity:* Starting a daily drawing practice

- *Community:* Organizing neighborhood clean-ups

_____

_____

_____

_____

_____

**Set SMART goals.** Select an activity for each value that feels achievable and meaningful, using SMART goals. SMART means that your goals are:

- *Specific:* Consist of clearly defined actions

- *Measurable:* You can track youe progress

- *Achievable:* Realistic given your resources

- *Relevant:* Aligned with your values

- *Time-bound:* Occur within a clear timeframe

**Create an action**. Break down each goal into actionable steps. Assign dates and times to each action step to stay accountable.

**Anticipate and overcome obstacles**. Think about what might prevent you from achieving your goals. Plan how to address these challenges.

**Take action**. Start engaging in the activities you've outlined. Keep a journal to record your experiences, feelings, and any adjustments you make.

**Reflect and adjust.** Set aside time each week to reflect on your progress. Possible reflection questions:

- How did engaging in this activity make me feel?

- What positive changes have I noticed?

- Were there unexpected challenges or rewards?

Adjust your goals if necessary. It's okay to modify your goals based on your experiences.

**Celebrate your achievements.** Recognize and celebrate the steps you've taken, no matter how small. Consider sharing your accomplishments with a trusted person or community for additional support and encouragement.

# CHAPTER 8

# Over the Long Term

Before we dive into the deeper process of long-term integration, it's helpful to first understand some of the key areas where psychedelic experiences can lead to growth. Recognizing these areas is essential because it allows you to reflect on your own experience and consider which aspects may be most relevant to your personal journey. This awareness can serve as a foundation for reflecting on how your life has shifted and where further integration work might be needed. Once you've explored these areas, we will move into a discussion about the long-term integration process—how to maintain and deepen these changes over months or even years after the initial experience.

# Five Key Areas for Growth

Research and lived experiences show that psychedelic journeys often have profound and lasting impacts on several areas of personal growth. We have identified five key domains where individuals commonly experience positive transformation: enhanced self-awareness, emotional healing, empathy, creativity, and mental health improvements.

## Self-Awareness

One of the most significant impacts is the potential for deep personal insight (Mograbi et al. 2024). During a psychedelic experience, many individuals report a shift in their sense of self (Fischman 2019), leading to a heightened understanding of repressed emotions and subconscious patterns (Buchborn et al. 2023). This increase in self-awareness often sets the stage for emotional healing and greater alignment with one's authentic self.

## Emotion Regulation

Psychedelics also offer a powerful tool for processing and healing from emotional wounds (Thiessen et al. 2018). By dissolving barriers and defenses, these experiences allow individuals to confront past events or unresolved feelings (Buchborn et al. 2023). The result can lead to improved emotional well-being and a sense of liberation.

## Empathy and Interconnectedness

A profound sense of interconnectedness with others and the world often emerges during a psyche-delic experience (Blatchford, Bright, and Engel 2021; Kałużna et al. 2022). This expanded empathy reduces feelings of isolation and can foster more meaningful, compassionate relationships. It can also cultivate a greater sense of purpose and belonging, especially for those dealing with mental health challenges such as depression and anxiety (Móró et al. 2011).

## Creativity

Creativity and problem-solving abilities may be enhanced as psychedelic experiences open up new ways of thinking (Baggott 2015; Costa 2023). Whether in the arts, sciences, or everyday problem-solving, many individuals find themselves more able to tap into innovative ideas and perspectives after a psychedelic journey.

## Mental Health Benefits

Besides these subjective areas of growth, psychedelics have been found to help alleviate symptoms of depression (Wheeler and Dyer 2020), anxiety (Ko et al. 2023), PTSD (Mitchell et al. 2023), and addiction (Zafar et al. 2023). The ability of psychedelics to disrupt negative thought patterns and offer a fresh perspective on life has shown remarkable therapeutic potential.

At the end of this chapter, you'll find an exercise that is designed to help you explore and deepen the insights gained from your psychedelic experiences by focusing on five key areas of growth. It may help you identify which areas may require further integration or support.

# The Path of Long-Term Integration

People often find that it can take years to fully integrate the meaning of a psychedelic experience, as the impacts can be profound and far-reaching. In fact, participants in early psilocybin studies have reported that their psychedelic journey ranked among the five most important events in their lives (Carbonaro et al. 2016). Another study highlighted the potential for long-lasting personality changes, particularly increased openness, as a result of a psilocybin experience (MacLean, Johnson, and Griffiths 2011). As we delve into the long-term process of integration, it's important to recognize that the effects of a psychedelic experience may unfold gradually over months or even years, requiring ongoing reflection, support, and effort to fully incorporate the lessons into daily life. The following section explores some of the challenges and strategies involved in maintaining and deepening this integration over the long term.

In the days and weeks following a psychedelic experience, it's best not to make any drastic changes to your life right away. While there can be important exceptions—such as leaving an abusive relationship—most people are encouraged to give themselves time before making significant life decisions like changing jobs or filing for divorce. This period of waiting, often 3–6 months, serves as a safeguard against impulsive decisions, allowing space to fully consider the potential consequences of a big life change.

So when and how should these major decisions take place? It may be months or even years before the most challenging aspects of integration can emerge. Take, for example, the decision to end a marriage. In the early stages, this idea may have been a distant possibility, but as time progresses, it becomes a reality. Suddenly, one is faced with the tangible consequences: legal paperwork, meetings with attorneys, and navigating the emotional complexities of separation. While these struggles aren't directly tied to the psychedelic experience itself, the inner strength or courage needed to make such a decision may have originated from it. In these moments, the support of family, friends, or a psychotherapist becomes invaluable, just as it would during any major life transition.

Another common scenario involves someone who made positive strides in the weeks after their psychedelic journey, perhaps by addressing an issue like alcohol misuse. Over time, the challenge shifts to maintaining those gains and continuing to live out those changes. A useful framework for understanding this process is the **Stages of Change**, a **transtheoretical model** put forth by two psychotherapy researchers deeply involved in changes processes in addiction work (Prochaska and Norcross 2001). During long-term integration, we focus on the **maintenance stage**, where an individual has made important changes and is working to sustain them while avoiding a return to old habits.

Long-term integration requires awareness. After months of sustained change, it's easy to become complacent and assume the work is finished. However, true transformation takes time and consistent attention. At the same time, it's essential to avoid being too rigid. Recognizing and celebrating milestones along the way can help reinforce your progress. Reflecting on how far you've come serves as a reminder that integration is an ongoing process that continues to unfold.

As time passes, one of the specific challenges in long-term integration becomes the feeling of distance from the original psychedelic experience. The intensity and clarity of the journey may naturally fade, leaving a sense of disconnection. It's important to recognize that, while the psychedelic may have initiated the change, it is *you* who has done the hard work of transformation. If you feel a desire to reconnect with the experience, an exercise included below may help guide your decision. However, it's worth remembering that there are other ways to revisit the experience—through meditation, creative expression, or other contemplative practices.

Here is an exercise designed to help you support yourself through the maintenance phase of long-term integration. This exercise provides strategies to sustain the positive changes you've made.

# Self-Reflection Writing Prompts for
# Psychedelic Experiences

**Personal Insight and Self-Awareness.** Reflect on a specific psychedelic experience in which you felt a deep connection to your inner self.

- What new insights about your personality or behaviors did you gain during this time?

- Describe any repressed emotions or traumas that surfaced during your experience. How did confronting these aspects of yourself impact your emotional well-being and self-understanding?

- Consider how your sense of self has evolved since your psychedelic experience. In what ways has your self-awareness improved?

_____

_____

_____

_____

_____

_____

**Interconnectedness and Unity.** Think about a moment during a psychedelic journey when you felt a profound sense of unity with the world or people around you.

- How has this experience changed the way you view your relationships?

- Reflect on any feelings of isolation you had before your experience. Did the sense of interconnectedness you felt during your journey help alleviate these feelings? How?

- Describe how your understanding of others has changed since your psychedelic experience. Can you provide specific examples of how this newfound empathy has affected your interactions and relationships?

_____

_____

_____

_____

_____

_____

**Creativity and Cognitive Flexibility.** Recall any psychedelic experience that sparked a surge of creativity or new ways of thinking.

- How did this experience influence your approach to problem-solving or artistic endeavors?

- Reflect on any creative projects or solutions that emerged as a result of your experience. How did the psychedelic journey contribute to these innovations?

- Consider the ways in which your cognitive flexibility has been enhanced. How has this improved your ability to adapt to new situations or think outside the box?

_____

_____

_____

_____

_____

**Mental Health and Emotional Healing.** Reflect on any mental health challenges you faced prior to your psychedelic experience. Did you have depression, anxiety, PTSD, or addiction?

- How did your journey change your symptoms?

- Describe any negative thought patterns that were changed by your experience. Has this shift led to long-term improvements in your mental health?

- Think about the emotional healing you have experienced. What specific aspects of the psychedelic journey contributed most to this healing process?

_____

_____

_____

_____

_____

_____

**Spiritual Growth and Connection.** Recall any moment during your psychedelic experience when you felt a deep spiritual connection.

- How has this experience influenced your spiritual beliefs or practices?

- Reflect on any feelings of peace, gratitude, or awe you experienced. How have these feelings persisted in your daily life since the journey?

- Consider how your sense of purpose or understanding of your place in the universe has been affected. How has this spiritual growth contributed to your overall well-being?

_____

_____

_____

_____

_____

# Returning to the Medicine

The phrase **returning to the medicine** refers to the practice of using a psychedelic again after an initial transformative experience. As noted, psychedelic journeys can be deeply impactful, offering profound insights and healing. However, just like any therapeutic or spiritual practice, it can take more than a single session to fully integrate and benefit from these experiences.

The idea of returning to the medicine comes from traditional practices of indigenous cultures that have used psychedelic plants and fungi in their spiritual and healing rituals for centuries. These cultures often regard psychedelics as sacred medicines, tools for ongoing spiritual growth, and tools for emotional healing. Modern psychedelic therapy is contending with this question. We recognize that a single session can be a catalyst for change, but multiple sessions might be necessary to achieve deeper, sustained transformation. Read over the following section before deciding whether to have another experience. You may also wish to discuss this with your therapist or facilitator.

## When to Consider Having Another Psychedelic Experience

You may wish to embark on another psychedelic experience for any of these reasons:

**Further integration and healing.** After an initial experience, individuals may feel the need to delve deeper into unresolved issues or explore new layers of their psyche. Returning to the medicine can provide an opportunity for further healing and insight.

**Spiritual growth.** For those on a spiritual path, regular engagement with psychedelics can aid in deepening their connection to their spiritual beliefs and practices. It can be a way to continually renew and deepen their sense of purpose and connection to the divine or the universe.

**Mental health maintenance.** Psychedelics have shown promise in treating depression, anxiety, PTSD, and addiction. In some cases, periodic sessions can help maintain the therapeutic benefits and prevent relapse.

## When to Avoid Repeating the Experience

If any of the following apply, it might be better not to try another psychedelic experience—at least for now.

**Lack of grounding.** If an individual has not returned to a grounded, baseline state after their previous psychedelic experience, using psychedelics again too soon can lead to confusion and overwhelm. Getting grounded after an experience usually takes a day or two. The process usually is relatively smooth, but sometimes days later people feel like they are still not grounded and are not able to get back to normal daily routines. Integration involves reflecting on the insights gained and applying them to daily life, and may not feel complete for years. A person does not necessarily have to fully integrate each experience before the next, but should at least become grounded in daily life before using psychedelics again.

**Psychological instability**. When someone has a significant mental health crisis, such as severe depression, psychosis, or mania, returning to the medicine can make those symptoms worse. Remember, psychedelics can intensify emotions and perceptions, which may be harmful if the individual is not in a stable mental state.

**Dependence and escapism**. Some individuals might use psychedelics as a means of escaping reality, rather than confronting it. This can lead to psychological dependence and hinder personal growth, especially if the person relies on the substance for comfort rather than as an aid to addressing underlying issues.

**Physical health concerns**. Certain health conditions or medications can interact negatively with psychedelics. It is crucial to consider any potential physical health risks and consult with a healthcare professional before returning to the medicine.

Returning to the medicine is a nuanced practice that can offer profound benefits when approached thoughtfully and responsibly. Originating in a blend of ancient traditions and modern therapeutic practices, this practice recognizes the need for ongoing engagement to achieve sustained healing and growth. However, it is essential to ensure that the individual is in a stable mental and physical state and has adequately integrated their previous experiences.

The following exercise is designed to support your long-term integration process by focusing on the maintenance stage of change.

## Sustaining Long-Term Integration

**Reflection Journal (Continual Reflection).** Set aside 20–30 minutes to reflect on the lessons and insights from your psychedelic experience. Refer to previous exercises from other chapters, examining beliefs and values.

Consider the following questions. Write your answers down, if you like.

- What key takeaways from your experience still resonate with you today?

- How have those insights shaped your daily life, relationships, or worldview?

- Are there any aspects of the experience that have faded or feel distant? How might you reconnect with them?

- What new perspectives have emerged since your initial integration period?

Repeat this reflection once a month to keep the experience evolving.

_____

_____

_____

_____

_____

_____

_____

_____

**Developing Supportive Practices.** Reflect on your current self-care or maintenance practices. These may have been inspired by exercises in the previous chapters. Write down the practices you're currently engaging in that help maintain your integration.

- Are these practices working for you? If not, what adjustments can you make?

- Choose one new supportive practice you want to explore over the next month (for instance, a new type of meditation, a hobby, or a form of creative expression).

Make a plan to incorporate this new practice into your routine, even if just once a week.

_____

_____

_____

_____

**Relapse prevention.** Relapse doesn't just mean returning to unhealthy habits, it can also mean slipping back into old, limiting thought patterns or neglecting self-care. Reflect on any old patterns of thinking or behavior that have resurfaced since your psychedelic experience.

- Are there signs of drift (like avoiding self-care or engaging in toxic relationships)?

- What are three warning signs that signal you're moving away from the changes you've made to integrate?

_____

_____

_____

- Write down strategies to help you course-correct if you notice these warning signs (for example, reaching out to a friend, scheduling a therapy session, or practicing mindfulness).

_____

_____

_____

_____

**Adapting to new challenges.** Life will inevitably bring new stressors and challenges. This exercise helps you adapt lessons from your psychedelic experience to new circumstances.

- Think of a current challenge or stressor you are facing.

- Reflect on your psychedelic experience. What lessons or insights from that experience could help you approach this challenge?

- Write down how you can apply those insights to your current situation.

_____

_____

_____

_____

**Integration as a lifelong process.** It can be helpful to remember that change is an ongoing journey.

- Reflect on your growth since your psychedelic experience. What long-term changes have you made that align with your insights?

  _____

  _____

  _____

  _____

- What are some areas where you feel you can still grow or apply your insights in new ways?

  _____

  _____

  _____

  _____

- Consider how you can remain open to learning new lessons, even years after the experience.

  _____

  _____

  _____

  _____

Commit to revisiting this exercise periodically, perhaps once every six months, to assess your long-term integration process.

**Community connection.** Maintaining connection with a community can be a powerful support for your integration process.

- Reflect on your current community. Are you connected to others who support your integration process? If not, where could you find a group that shares similar values or experiences?

- If you are not already involved in an integration circle or community, identify one action you can take to connect with like-minded individuals. This could be joining an integration group, attending a retreat, or starting a monthly check-in with friends who have undergone similar experiences. You'll find some of these in the resource section of the workbook.

  _____

  _____

  _____

  _____

- Set a goal to reach out to someone in your community to discuss your integration process.

**Celebrate your progress.** Take a moment to celebrate how far you've come since your psychedelic experience.

- Write down three specific ways your life has changed for the better because of the work you've done to integrate the experience.

  _____

  _____

  _____

- Reflect on a personal milestone in your integration journey. How does it feel to acknowledge this growth?

  _____

  _____

  _____

  _____

- Consider ways to celebrate your progress, whether through a personal ritual, sharing your journey with a friend, or simply treating yourself to something meaningful.

# Using Psychedelic Inspiration for Positive Social Change

Psychedelic experiences often leave individuals profoundly inspired and transformed, prompting them to seek ways to contribute to positive social change. This inspiration can manifest in various forms, from promoting access to psychedelic therapy to engaging in broader social justice and community-building efforts. We've seen former patients go on to create advocacy organizations, educational programs, and clinics and aftercare services, as well as make a variety of other meaningful contributions to the field. One of the most direct ways to contribute is by becoming involved in the movement to promote access to psychedelic therapy.

Ways to get involved include:

- **Education and awareness:** Sharing personal stories and scientific research about the benefits of psychedelics can help reduce stigma and increase public understanding. Hosting workshops, writing articles, or giving talks can be powerful ways to educate others.

- **Supporting clinical research:** Volunteering or donating to organizations conducting clinical trials on psychedelics can help advance scientific knowledge and pave the way for legal therapeutic use.

- **Training and certification:** Becoming a certified psychedelic therapist or guide can enable individuals to provide direct support to those seeking healing through these substances, ensuring safe and effective experiences.

Another significant way to build on inspiration is by engaging in advocacy and policy work aimed at reforming laws and regulations surrounding psychedelic substances. This can involve:

- **Lobbying and legislation:** Working with local, state, or national legislators to advocate for policy changes that decriminalize psychedelics and support their medical use. Participating in lobbying efforts, drafting policy proposals, and building coalitions can drive legislative progress.

- **Grassroots movements:** Joining or organizing grassroots movements to campaign for the rights of individuals to access psychedelic therapies. This can include organizing petitions, marches, or public demonstrations to raise awareness and pressure policymakers.

- **Nonprofit organizations:** Contributing to or working with nonprofits dedicated to drug policy reform, mental health advocacy, and public education on psychedelics can amplify efforts to create systemic change.

Inspired by the sense of interconnectedness and empathy often experienced during psychedelic journeys, individuals can also channel their energy into broader social justice and community-building initiatives, including:

- **Mental health advocacy:** Promoting mental health awareness and support can have a far-reaching impact. This can include volunteering at mental health organizations, providing peer support, or advocating for better mental health services in underserved communities.

- **Environmental activism:** Many people feel a deep connection to nature during psychedelic experiences, inspiring them to protect the environment. Engaging in conservation efforts, supporting sustainable practices, or participating in environmental activism can help preserve the planet for future generations.

- **Creative and artistic contributions:** Use your newfound creativity to produce art, music, literature, or other forms of expression that inspire and uplift others. Artistic endeavors can raise awareness about important issues, foster community, and promote cultural change.

- **Community service:** Consider volunteering time and skills to support local communities, whether through organizing community events, supporting local charities, or helping those in need. Acts of service can strengthen community bonds and create a more compassionate society.

In summary, individuals inspired by their psychedelic experiences have a wide array of avenues to contribute to positive social change. From promoting access to psychedelic therapy and engaging in advocacy and policy work to participating in broader social justice and community-building efforts, the potential for impact is vast. By harnessing the insights and empathy gained from these experiences, people can help build a more understanding, compassionate, and just world. The next exercise can help you choose your own form of advocacy.

# Identifying Your Path to Contribution

First, think about what you are already good at. Elaborate on at least three skills you possess that have served you well in your career or family or as a volunteer in the past. For example, under "organizational" you might write "I am good with spreadsheets" or "I'm always the one who makes the lists of what we'll need."

Communication: _____

_____

_____

Organizational: _____

_____

_____

Leadership: _____

_____

_____

Technical: _____

_____

_____

Research: _____

_____

_____

Other areas: _____

_____

_____

Now, elaborate on at least three areas of interest you have outside of psychedelics:

Environment and conservation: _____

_____

_____

Health and wellness: _____

_____

_____

Policy and advocacy: _____

_____

_____

Education: _____

_____

_____

Arts and culture: _____

_____

_____

Other areas: _____

_____

_____

Next, use your preferred search engine or social media platform to search for organizations that combine your area of interest with psychedelics. For example, if you selected arts and culture and searched for "psychedelic art and culture," you might come across the Psychedelic Art and Culture Trust. Fill in the organizations you find below, visit their websites, and read their mission statements. If listed, look at who is on their leadership team and find out more about those individuals. Maybe you will even see a name you recognize or someone you already know! If they have a mailing list or social media channel, sign up and follow along. You may even find an event, webinar, or conference to attend and learn more.

My psychedelic organizations of interest and their leaders are:

- **Organization 1:** _____

  Leader: _____

  Leader: _____

  Leader: _____

- **Organization 2:** _____

  Leader: _____

  Leader: _____

  Leader: _____

- **Organization 3:** _____

  Leader: _____

  Leader: _____

  Leader: _____

After you've spent some time following an organization's work and learning about it, go back to the skills you identified and think about how you might contribute to the organization. Reach out and ask what help they might need. Tell them the skills you have and be sure to identify what interests you most about the organization's work. Keep in mind many organizations in the psychedelics world are very small and run by just a few staff members or volunteers, so there may be limited resources for new projects. But your genuine interest and offer to help will surely be appreciated, even if there isn't a current fit for your skills. Most importantly, keep searching and following and staying connected to the field until you find the right fit.

# Conclusion

The journey to using psychedelics in clinical research and therapy has followed a long and sometimes rocky road. Early research stalled in the face of popular and political backlash, denying generations of researchers the opportunity to capitalize on past progress. But after a long struggle, psychedelic research has returned and is making strides in showing the great potential of psychedelics in treating a variety of mental disorders.

There are many types of psychedelics, and different types may have very different effects. It is vital that you understand the effects and potential dangers of any psychedelic that you are considering for use. It is also vital to understand the federal and state laws regarding psychedelics. The legal landscape surrounding psychedelic use in the United States can be confusing. Federal law predominates, but each state and territory can have laws of their own regarding psychedelics. While psychedelics are strictly illegal in many places, some states and cities have decriminalized or deprioritized certain psychedelics (but perhaps not others). Before proceeding with any use of psychedelics, consult the relevant federal laws and the laws of your state or territory. The penalties for breaking these laws are often quite substantial.

No matter how you may have heard of psychedelics, the decision to use them is a deeply personal one. It is important that you understand your motives and desires in seeking out a psychedelic experience. Study your personal pros and cons regarding use to make an intelligent decision as to whether to proceed. If you choose to proceed, it's a very good idea to do so under the observation of a professional trained in psychedelic treatment or someone with training or experience in accompanying those engaged in a psychedelic experience.

Thoughtful preparation will increase your likelihood of deriving benefits from your experience, as well as decrease your likelihood of having a negative psychedelic experience. The information and exercises in this book will aid you in preparing for your experience and in coping with any difficulties you may encounter.

Having the proper mindset, as well as a comfortable and safe setting for your psychedelic experience, are important components to ensuring your best possible experience. During and after your experience, you will likely encounter unpredictable and sometimes profound emotional and perceptual changes. Important insights may arrive suddenly and result in a rapid change in mental state, behavior, and overall well-being. While such abrupt changes may sound alarming, the result can be lasting gains in self-awareness, meaning, connection, and mental health condition. It is important to refrain from resisting or judging what you feel during an experience, but rather embrace it and let it unfold as it will, revealing deeper layers of your psyche and allowing organic insights and transformations to surface.

Before you proceed, it's a good idea to set your intentions for your experience. However, it's best to hold these intentions loosely and not try to bend your experience to fit into their framework. Greater insight can be gained by allowing the experience to unfold naturally. Meet the experience with openness and curiosity and allow yourself to accept what it reveals.

You may find your experience to be difficult, or you may feel that nothing has happened at all. Most difficult experiences can be navigated by traveling in and through. Let yourself feel the difficult sensations rather than trying to change or control them. If you cannot go in and through, utilize the tools you developed in this handbook to weather the storm. If it seems that your experience could be summed up in the words "nothing happened," remember that even an uneventful journey has value from which insights can be gained.

After your psychedelic journey, you begin to integrate its insights into your life. You may have received a large amount of insight in the few hours of your experience, but integrating that insight will take time. Be patient, as this may take days or considerably longer. Confiding in a trusted friend or family member could be helpful in integrating your insights, so long as that person is nonjudgmental, open-minded, and willing to listen, and you can talk in a place that makes you feel safe and secure. If you have serious difficulties after your experience, it would be best to seek help from a professional who is knowledgeable about psychedelics.

Should you choose to engage in a psychedelic experience, your journey of discovery and integration will be a personal one. No one can say just how it will unfold or what insights it will bring you. Prepare for the experience so that it will be a safe and beneficial one. Meet the experience with openness and curiosity to glean all of the insights you can. Be patient and self-compassionate as you integrate your insights into your life and grow from the lessons to be learned. Work through any difficulties and don't be afraid to ask for help if you need it. Immerse yourself in your journey as it happens and when it's over, allow yourself to learn the lessons it has to teach. Utilize its insights to make yourself healthier, happier, and more satisfied in life.

# Acknowledgments

We acknowledge the influences of early psychedelic therapy researchers, cultural anthropologists and historians, and indigenous communities that have all contributed to our understanding of the myriad ways that psychedelics are used. We acknowledge the contributions of drug policy researchers, harm reduction advocates, and pioneering psychotherapists who have challenged the status quo of health care and provided services to those who were traditionally marginalized and excluded from such systems due to their personal choice to use psychedelic drugs. Locating psychedelic therapy practices, including PHRI, in the cultural and historical context in which they stand is critical to providing ethical, trauma-informed care.

We are exceptionally grateful for the entire team at Fluence, whose tireless dedication and professionalism move the world toward greater acceptance of psychedelic therapies every single day. In addition, we acknowledge and thank our colleagues at MAPS and Lykos for leading the charge to destigmatize psychedelic therapy through research and regulatory approval. We honor all of our community partnership organizations engaged in education, advocacy, and harm reduction work, including Chacruna, Fireside Project, Black Therapists Rock, National Psychedelics Association, Psychedelic Medicine Association, Reason for Hope, and so many more. Finally, we thank our editors at New Harbinger who sought to bring this book into existence and supported its creation and publication with invaluable feedback along the way.

# Glossary

**3,4-methylenedioxymethamphetamine:** Known as MDMA or Ecstasy; a synthetic drug with stimulant and empathogenic properties.

**Acetylcholine receptors:** Proteins that respond to the neurotransmitter acetylcholine, involved in transmitting nerve signals.

**Adulterant:** a substance added to another to increase its volume or change its quality, such as watering down milk or wine.

**Adulterated:** When a substance is added to another substance that weakens it or reduces its quality.

**Agency:** In mental health, an individual's capacity to make choices, take action, and exert control over their own life, reflecting empowerment and autonomy.

**Agonist:** A substance that initiates a response when it binds to a receptor on a neuron.

**Alkaloid:** An organic compound found in plants containing nitrogen atoms, often affecting human and animal physiology.

**Alpha-alkyl chain:** Carbon atoms attached to the alpha position of a molecule, adjacent to a functional group.

**Anesthetic:** A substance that causes loss of sensation to prevent pain during medical procedures.

**Antagonism:** In chemistry, inhibition or blocking of certain functions.

**Aromatic ring:** A chemical compound that is highly stable.

**Arylcyclohexylamine:** A chemical class of drugs, including phencyclidine (PCP), known for dissociative and anesthetic properties.

**Autonomy:** The freedom to make one's own choices.

**Ayahuasca:** A hallucinogenic brew made from Amazonian plants, traditionally used by indigenous shamans in rituals.

**Bad trip:** A distressing psychedelic experience characterized by intense fear, anxiety, confusion, or negative emotions.

**Being vs. doing:** Being in the moment rather than performing actions during a psychedelic experience.

**Beta-carbolines:** Compounds found in plants and animals that inhibit monoamine oxidase enzymes and may have psychoactive effects.

**Biopsychosocial:** A model considering biological, psychological, and social factors as interconnected influences on an individual's well-being.

**Bicyclic hexahydroindole ring fused to a bicyclic quinoline group:** In LSD, a complex structure where two-ring systems (hexahydroindole and quinoline) are fused together.

**Breakthrough therapy:** An FDA designation for substances that show promise to be more useful than current treatments.

**Cannabidiol:** A non-psychoactive compound in cannabis plants, known for potential therapeutic benefits like reducing anxiety and inflammation.

**Cannabis:** A plant genus producing psychoactive compounds, used for medicinal and recreational purposes.

**Central nervous system:** Comprises the brain and spinal cord; controls the body's activities and processes information from the senses.

**Chemistry:** The study of the elements that make up matter, such as atoms and molecules.

**Chiral structure:** A molecular structure existing in two mirror-image forms (enantiomers).

**Cognition:** Mental processes involved in acquiring knowledge, including thinking, remembering, and problem-solving.

**Decriminalized:** When criminal penalties are removed from an action; it remains illegal but is not prosecuted as a crime.

**Delirium:** A serious disturbance in mental abilities, leading to confused thinking and reduced awareness of the environment.

**Derealization:** A dissociative symptom where the external world feels unreal or distorted.

**Deprioritized:** Assigned a lower level of importance or priority.

**Dimethyltryptamine:** Also known as DMT; a powerful psychedelic compound found in various plants and animals.

**Diterpenoid:** Chemical compound derived from plants, consisting of four isoprene units; usually found in gums and resins.

**Dopamine:** A neurotransmitter affecting attention, memory, movement, motivation, and mood.

**Effectiveness:** How well a drug or treatment works in real-world settings, where conditions are less controlled. It reflects the actual benefit to patients when used in typical clinical practice. Contrasted with efficacy, which refers to how well a drug or treatment works under ideal and controlled conditions, such as in clinical trials.

**Ego dissolution:** The loss of one's sense of self; not seeing oneself as a separate being from others.

**Embodied integration:** Incorporating insights from a psychedelic experience into one's physical and emotional awareness for meaningful application in daily life.

**Empathogens:** Psychoactive drugs that induce feelings of emotional communion, oneness, and empathy; also known as entactogens. They increase the ability to understand and share the emotions of others, promoting social bonding and improved interpersonal communication.

**Entactogens:** Psychoactive substances that promote introspection and enhance one's ability to access and reflect upon personal emotions, fostering inner peace and self-understanding. They facilitate a deep connection with one's own thoughts and feelings.

**Ergolines:** Compounds derived from ergot alkaloids, sometimes possessing medicinal or psychedelic properties.

**Ergot alkaloids:** Alkaloids derived from a fungus on rye, capable of causing hallucinations and muscle spasms.

**Excitatory neurotransmitter:** A chemical messenger that increases the likelihood of a neuron firing.

**GABA receptors:** Proteins responding to the neurotransmitter GABA, typically reducing neuronal excitability.

**Glutamate:** The primary excitatory neurotransmitter that enhances neuronal firing.

**Harmala alkaloids:** Compounds in certain plants that inhibit monoamine oxidase enzymes and may have psychoactive effects.

**In and through:** Allowing experiences during a psychedelic session to unfold without attempting to control them.

**Indigenous:** Originating or occurring naturally in a specific place; native populations or cultures.

**Indolealkylamine:** Chemical derivatives of serotonin capable of causing hallucinations and sensory distortions.

**Inner-directed experience:** Focusing inward during a psychedelic session to explore personal thoughts and emotions.

**Intergenerational trauma:** Psychological trauma handed down from one generation to the next; for example, the inherited trauma of enslavement.

**Interpersonal sensitivity:** The ability to perceive and understand others' nonverbal cues and emotions.

**Kappa opioid receptor agonist:** A substance that activates kappa opioid receptors, influencing pain perception and mood.

**Legalized:** When an action or substance is made legal by law.

**Lysergic acid diethylamide:** Known as LSD, a potent synthetic psychedelic derived from ergot alkaloids.

**Maintenance stage:** In the Stages of Change model, the phase of sustaining behavior change and preventing relapse.

**Mania:** A mental state characterized by extreme energy, activity, and elevated mood.

**Medicalized:** Treating a previously nonmedical issue as a medical problem requiring intervention.

**Melatonin:** A hormone regulating sleep-wake cycles, produced by the pineal gland.

**Mescaline:** A natural psychedelic compound found in peyote and some other cacti.

**Metabolite:** A substance produced during metabolism, participating in further biochemical reactions.

**Methylenedioxy group:** A chemical group consisting of two oxygen atoms bonded to a carbon atom, forming a ring.

**Monoamine oxidase A:** An enzyme that breaks down neurotransmitters like serotonin and norepinephrine.

**Neoshamanic:** Blending ancient shamanic traditions with contemporary methods to promote healing and personal growth.

**Neuroplasticity:** The brain's ability to adapt, reorganize, and form new neural connections.

**Neurotransmitter:** Chemical messengers transmitting signals between neurons across synapses.

**Neuroticism:** A personality trait involving a tendency toward negative emotions like anxiety, worry, fear, anger, or frustration.

**Nicotinic receptors:** Acetylcholine receptors responsive to nicotine, important in neural signaling.

**NMDA receptor:** A receptor on neurons that controls memory, learning, and neuroplasticity.

**Nonlinear change:** Psychological progress occurring in unpredictable, irregular patterns rather than a steady single direction.

**Norepinephrine:** A hormone and neurotransmitter involved in alertness and the fight-or-flight response.

**Off-label:** Using a drug to treat conditions other than those for which it is officially approved.

**Openness and curiosity:** Embracing a psychedelic experience without judgment or immediate interpretation.

**Opiates:** Natural alkaloids derived from opium poppies; used for pain relief but potentially highly addictive.

**Opioid:** A class of drugs acting on opioid receptors, including natural, synthetic, and semisynthetic compounds. Used primarily for pain relief but highly addictive. Some opioids are not used for pain, such as loperamide, an anti-diarrheal medication.

**Opioid receptors:** Proteins that bind opioids, mediating their effects on pain and reward.

**Orally active:** A substance effective when administered by mouth.

**Paranoia:** A persistent feeling of being persecuted or targeted.

**Peyote:** A small, spineless cactus containing mescaline, used in Native American spiritual practices.

**Pharmacological profile:** A comprehensive description of a drug's actions, effects, metabolism, and interactions.

**Pharmacology:** The study of interactions between chemical substances—whether naturally occurring, human-made, or semisynthesized—and the brain.

**Phenethylamines:** Compounds based on the phenethylamine structure, some acting as stimulants or hallucinogens.

**Phencyclidine:** Also known as PCP, a dissociative drug with mind-altering effects.

**Positive feedback loop:** Actions that elicit a response that affirms the value of the action.

**Post-traumatic stress disorder:** A mental health condition that develops after someone either witnesses or is part of a traumatic event.

**Practice-based:** Developed out of real-world experiences and client interactions.

**Prodrug:** A compound that is metabolized into an active drug within the body.

**Psilocybin:** A psychedelic compound in certain mushrooms, metabolized into psilocin in the body.

**Psychedelic-assisted psychotherapy:** Treatment combining psychedelics and psychotherapy in a controlled setting for lasting psychological change.

**Psychedelic therapy:** Same as psychedelic-assisted psychotherapy.

**Returning to the medicine:** Using a psychedelic again after an initial experience.

**Schedule 1:** A classification for substances with high abuse potential and no accepted medical use, per regulatory agencies.

**Semisynthetic:** Compounds chemically synthesized from natural substances.

**Serotonergic hallucinogens:** Substances that induce hallucinations primarily by acting on serotonin receptors.

**Serotonin:** A neurotransmitter that plays a role in many brain functions, including mood, cognition, learning, and memory. It is often referred to as the "feel good" hormone.

**Serotonin (5-HT) receptors:** Proteins that bind serotonin, involved in mood, appetite, and sleep regulation.

**Set:** Refers to an individual's mindset, including beliefs, expectations, and emotional state during a psychedelic experience.

**Set and setting:** The combination of one's mindset (set) and the environment (setting) during a psychedelic session, influencing the experience.

**Setting:** The physical and social environment where a psychedelic experience occurs, including relationships with facilitators.

**Setting an intention:** Defining reasons for use or areas for growth to guide one's psychedelic journey.

**Sigma receptors:** Proteins influencing mood, pain, and memory by regulating neurotransmitter systems.

**Stages of Change:** A model outlining the process of behavioral change through stages like contemplation and action.

**Substituted amphetamine:** Compounds based on amphetamine, including various stimulants and hallucinogens.

**Substituted methylenedioxyphenethylamine:** Chemical compounds derived from phenethylamines and that have psychedelic or stimulant properties.

**Supervised adult use:** Legal use of a substance by adults under professional supervision.

**Synthesized:** Produced through chemical synthesis; often replicating a natural product.

**Tetrahydrocannabinol:** Known as THC, the primary psychoactive component of cannabis.

**Thalidomide disaster:** In the mid-20th century, thalidomide was approved for use as a sedative in Canada and several European countries. It was prescribed to treat morning sickness without being tested in pregnant women. The result was thousand of miscarriages and severe birth defects in over 10,000 children—40 percent of whom died shortly after birth. Although the FDA refused to approve it for use in the United States, over a thousand doctors received samples directly from the pharmaceutical company and gave them to patients.

**Tolerance:** Reduced response to a drug after use, requiring higher doses for the same effect.

**Transtheoretical model:** A framework describing stages of behavioral change, integrating concepts from various therapies.

**Tryptamine structure:** A basic chemical pattern found in many natural substances, including important brain chemicals like serotonin and some plant compounds that can affect mood and perception. It consists of a ring-shaped part connected to a small chain of atoms, acting as a common building block in molecules that influence the brain

**Tryptamines:** Compounds with a tryptamine structure (see above), some with psychoactive effects.

**Underground practitioners (also called underground therapists):** Individuals offering psychedelic therapy outside of legal frameworks.

**Underwhelming experience:** A psychedelic experience that was less intense or impactful than expected.

**Unfolding process:** The spontaneous personal and spiritual growth that can occur naturally when individuals engage deeply with their inner experiences.

**Values-based action:** Taking actions aligned with one's core values, promoting a meaningful and purpose-driven life.

**Withdrawal:** Symptoms that occur after reducing or stopping a drug that one has become dependent on.

# Resources for Further Learning

Psychedelic research is an immense field these days. We suggest the following resources for reputable information about clinical studies, science, and policy.

**Beckley Foundation**

Website: beckleyfoundation.org

Noteworthy for: global psychedelic research, policy work, and pioneering scientific discoveries.

**Center for Psychedelic & Consciousness Research**

Website: hopkinspsychedelic.org

Noteworthy for: research and trials on psychedelics and mental health.

**Chacruna**

Website: chacruna.net

Noteworthy for: education, sociological perspectives, cross-cultural and indigenous knowledge.

**Drug Policy Alliance**

Website: drugpolicy.org

Noteworthy for: organization focusing on studying and decreasing the harms of drug prohibition.

## Drug Science

Website: drugscience.org.uk

Noteworthy for: independent, science-led charity providing information about drug effects.

## Fireside Project

Website: firesideproject.org

Noteworthy for: offering a free, confidential peer support hotline for people during or after psychedelic experiences.

## Fluence

Website: fluence.org

Noteworthy for: education, clinical training, webinars, and online courses.

## Food and Drug Administration

Website: fda.gov

Noteworthy for: regulatory updates, drug approvals, and guidelines related to psychedelics.

## Global Drug Survey

Website: globaldrugsurvey.com

Noteworthy for: worldwide surveys on drug use trends to inform public health policy.

## Heffter Research Institute

Website: heffter.org

Noteworthy for: research focused primarily on psilocybin for various mental health conditions.

## Imperial College London - Centre for Psychedelic Research

Website: psychedelicresearchcentre.com

Noteworthy for: cutting-edge research in neuroscientific and clinical aspects of psychedelics.

**International Center for Ethnobotanical Education Research and Services**

Website: iceers.org

Noteworthy for: integration of traditional knowledge and modern science, with a focus on ethnobotanical research.

**Multidisciplinary Association for Psychedelic Studies**

Website: maps.org

Noteworthy for: research, clinical trials, and advocacy related to psychedelic-assisted therapies.

**National Institute of Health - Clinical Trials**

Website: clinicaltrials.gov

Noteworthy for: a place to learn about clinical studies from around the world.

**Psychedelic Alpha**

Website: psychedelicalpha.com

Noteworthy for: updates on the psychedelic drug development industry, clinical trials tracker, and drug policy advancements in the US.

**Usona Institute**

Website: usonainstitute.org

Noteworthy for: clinical trials and research on psychedelic medicines.

**Zendo Project**

Website: zendoproject.org

Noteworthy for: providing harm reduction services and education at events where psychedelics are present, offering training on how to support individuals through challenging experiences.

# Case Studies

The following case examples will be helpful for clinicians who wish to see how the PHRI model works in clinical practice. These case examples each combine several typical scenarios we've seen in our practices and are not representative of any one single client's story. Read each example and think through the analyses provided. We suggest writing out your own impressions and thinking about any similar situations you might have seen in your clinical practice.

## Case Example 1

### Identifying Information

Sandra is a single woman in her late 40s who lives alone in an apartment in a large metropolitan area in the United States. Occasionally, she shares her apartment with a roommate to alleviate financial strain. Employed as a yoga teacher, Sandra sought therapy in my private practice for psychedelic integration after undergoing ketamine infusion treatment and participating in three ayahuasca ceremonies.

### Presenting Problem

In January 2020, Sandra presented for her initial intake, expressing that although her depressive symptoms and suicidal ideation had significantly improved following ketamine infusions and ayahuasca ceremonies, she was grappling with a profound identity crisis. She articulated, "I used to know exactly who I was with absolute certainty, which only comes from being depressed. Now that I'm not depressed, I don't know who I am." This statement encapsulated her confusion about navigating life without the familiar anchor of depression and her struggle to integrate her spiritual experiences into her daily existence.

At the outset of our work, Sandra's primary goal was to understand how to live as a nondepressed individual and to rediscover a sense of self amid her newfound wellness.

## Personal and Family History

Born in Warsaw, Poland, in 1976, Sandra is of Polish descent. She has one younger brother, born 16 months after her. Following her brother's birth, Sandra's mother suffered from severe postnatal depression. During this challenging period, her father began an affair but continued to reside in the family home without communicating with Sandra's mother for five years. When Sandra was six, her father moved out, and her parents divorced.

Sandra described her childhood relationship with her father as emotionally abusive. Her mother, coping with her own depression, often resorted to alcohol and cigarettes. Sandra felt her mother was unable to protect either of them from her father's abuse. Additionally, her younger brother was verbally abusive, frequently belittling her with statements like "You are fat, stupid, no one likes you."

Feeling unwelcome and unsupported, Sandra moved to the United States at age 27, hoping to escape her life in Poland. She characterized her family culture as reserved in emotional expression, dismissive of feelings, and skeptical of spirituality, which they regarded as impractical or frivolous.

## Past Psychiatric History

From a young age, Sandra experienced persistent sadness and grief. Over the years, she tried various psychiatric medications, including selective serotonin reuptake inhibitors, and engaged in psychotherapy but found no lasting relief. Her suicidal ideation worsened over the next period of her life, escalating from passive thoughts to active planning.

In October 2017, Sandra received ketamine infusion treatments. She reported an immediate and significant relief from her depressive symptoms and suicidal ideation. Her provider suggested that her symptoms were rooted in childhood PTSD. Initially skeptical, Sandra became convinced of the treatment's efficacy after maintaining remission for six months.

Seeking further help, she participated in three ayahuasca ceremonies between spring and summer 2018. These experiences led to an increased capacity for happiness and a profound sense of spiritual connectedness—a dramatic shift from her previously staunch atheism.

## Case Formulation

Sandra's case presents a complex interplay of biological, psychological, and social factors. Biologically, she has a history of treatment-resistant depression and may have a genetic predisposition to mood disorders. Psychologically, her childhood was marked by emotional abuse and neglect from both parents and her brother. This environment fostered anger, which she directed inward, leading to deep-seated self-negativity and a depressive identity that became integral to her sense of self.

Socially, Sandra lacked supportive family relationships and felt a pervasive sense of isolation. Her cultural background was reserved and often dismissive of emotional expression and spirituality, further inhibiting her ability to process her feelings and seek help. The rapid alleviation of her depressive symptoms through ketamine and ayahuasca disrupted her long-held identity as a depressed individual, plunging her into an identity crisis. She struggled with rejection sensitivity, finding it difficult to connect with others due to fear of further rejection—a fear reinforced by her family's negative reactions to her wellness.

Moreover, Sandra grappled with spiritual ambivalence. Her ayahuasca experiences awakened a spirituality that conflicted with her lifelong atheism. Integrating these new beliefs into her daily life proved challenging, as they were at odds with her cultural upbringing and her family's views.

The primary targets for intervention included helping Sandra reconstruct her identity beyond her depression, processing unresolved anger and grief related to her family, and integrating her spiritual experiences in a way that felt authentic and balanced.

## Course of Treatment

Over approximately nine months of weekly PHRI therapy, Sandra and I embarked on a journey to address her identity crisis and integrate her psychedelic experiences.

In the initial phase, establishing a strong therapeutic alliance was paramount. I provided a safe, nonjudgmental space where Sandra could openly discuss her psychedelic experiences and the disorientation she felt. Recognizing her confusion, I introduced the concept of **therapeutic bends**, explaining that rapid alleviation from depression can be unsettling and may require time to adjust. This normalization seemed to alleviate some of her anxiety.

To help her stay grounded, we incorporated mindfulness practices into our sessions. I guided her through grounding exercises aimed at enhancing her present-moment awareness and connection to her emotions. Sandra was receptive to these practices and began integrating them into her daily routine.

As we progressed into the middle phase of therapy, Sandra took us deeper into her childhood trauma. Utilizing relational techniques, we explored the impact of her parents' divorce, the emotional abuse from her father, and the neglect she experienced. Sandra began to uncover how these early experiences shaped her self-perception and relationships. Processing this trauma was emotionally challenging for her, but it led to significant insights.

Concurrent with this exploration, we used a nondirective approach that encouraged Sandra to tap into her inner wisdom to address her deep-seated self-criticisms stemming from her family's abuse. I invited Sandra to reflect on these beliefs at her own pace. Through open-ended questions and attentive listening, she began to uncover the origins of her self-criticisms. This process allowed Sandra to recognize the disconnect between her negative self-perceptions and her sense of self. As she connected with her innate capacity for self-compassion, Sandra became more aware of when she was engaging in negative self-talk and started to naturally cultivate a kinder, more understanding view of herself.

Integration of her spiritual experiences was another critical aspect of our work. Sandra shared her ayahuasca experiences and her subsequent exploration of spiritual philosophies such as Buddhism. She expressed both fascination and confusion about these new beliefs. I encouraged her to discuss these insights, helping her find personal meaning and reconcile these new beliefs with her identity. Validating her spiritual journey seemed to reduce her feelings of isolation, as she felt understood and accepted.

In the later phase of therapy, we focused on enhancing her interpersonal relationships. Sandra often felt disconnected from others and feared rejection. We practiced interpersonal effectiveness skills, such as assertive communication and active listening, to improve her interactions. She began to reach out more, participating in community activities like volunteering at a community garden, which provided a sense of belonging.

We also developed a relapse prevention plan. Recognizing that future stressors could challenge her mood, we identified coping strategies and support systems she could rely on. Sandra expressed confidence in her ability to maintain her progress but acknowledged the importance of ongoing effort.

Throughout the therapy, Sandra was highly engaged and motivated. She embraced mindfulness and meditation, finding them instrumental in managing her emotions. Discussing her spiritual beliefs within therapy provided a sanctuary where she could explore and integrate these concepts without judgment.

## Outcome and Prognosis

By the conclusion of our work together, Sandra had made significant strides. She maintained remission from depression, with no recurrence of depressive symptoms or suicidal ideation. Her self-perception shifted as she developed an identity not defined by depression but enriched by her experiences and personal growth.

Sandra repaired her relationship with her father, initiating contact and finding her feelings reciprocated. Her connection with her mother also strengthened, providing a supportive familial bond she had previously lacked. While her relationship with her brother remained strained, brief amicable communications had resumed, and she reported a reduction in intrusive thoughts about him.

Socially, Sandra became more engaged. She began dating and sought opportunities to connect with others who shared her interests, mitigating her feelings of isolation. Volunteering and attending community events contributed to a sense of purpose and belonging.

She successfully integrated her spiritual insights into her daily life, finding a balance that resonated with her. Sandra continued her meditation practice and remained involved with the Buddhist center, which provided both spiritual fulfillment and social connection.

The prognosis for Sandra is cautiously optimistic. She has demonstrated resilience and a capacity for self-reflection. Continued practice of mindfulness, engagement in meaningful activities, and utilization of her support network are recommended to sustain her well-being.

## Diagnostic Impressions (DSM-5)

- Persistent Depressive Disorder (Dysthymia), in Full Remission (F34.1)

- Post-Traumatic Stress Disorder (F43.10)

- Unspecified Personality Disorder with Dependent and Avoidant Features (F60.9)

## Relevance to Broader Practice

Sandra's case underscores the complexities that can arise when rapid symptom relief occurs through psychedelic treatments. While alleviation of depression is a positive outcome, it can precipitate an identity crisis, as the individual may have been anchored to their symptoms for a significant period. This highlights the necessity of providing supportive integration therapy to help clients navigate these transitions.

The integration of spiritual experiences into therapy is also a crucial consideration. Clinicians should remain open and nonjudgmental, validating clients' beliefs and assisting them in finding personal meaning. This approach can reduce feelings of isolation and enhance therapeutic outcomes.

Sandra's journey illustrates the effectiveness of combining psychodynamic exploration with PHRI techniques. Addressing deep-seated emotional issues through this integrated approach can facilitate profound healing and personal growth.

Cultural sensitivity is essential, particularly when clients come from backgrounds that stigmatize emotional expression and spirituality. Understanding these cultural influences can help clinicians tailor interventions that respect the client's worldview while promoting healing.

## Ethical Considerations

Confidentiality was strictly maintained throughout treatment. All identifying information was altered to protect Sandra's privacy. Informed consent was obtained, and Sandra was fully informed about the therapeutic approaches utilized. A nonjudgmental stance was maintained at all times, providing a safe environment for Sandra to explore her experiences without fear of stigma or judgment.

# Case Example 2

## Identifying Information

Carlos is a man in his late 50s who lives with his wife in a suburban area of a large metropolitan city in the United States. They have two adult children who have moved out and live independently. Carlos has been a high school teacher for over 30 years. He sought therapy in my private practice to explore the possibility of using psychedelics for personal growth and to address longstanding feelings of dissatisfaction.

## Presenting Problem

In January 2023, Carlos presented for his initial intake, expressing uncertainty about whether he should have a psychedelic experience. He had never used psychedelics before but had recently become curious about their potential benefits. Carlos stated, "I've been feeling stuck for a while now. I've heard that psychedelics can help people gain new perspectives, but I'm not sure if it's right for me." He sought professional guidance to explore his motivations and make an informed decision.

At the outset of our work, Carlos's primary goal was to understand the potential risks and benefits of psychedelics and to determine whether pursuing such an experience aligned with his personal values and circumstances.

## Personal and Family History

Born in Mexico City in 1965, Carlos is of Mexican descent. He is the eldest of five siblings. His family immigrated to the United States when he was ten years old, seeking better economic opportunities. Carlos described his upbringing as traditional, emphasizing hard work, family unity, and adherence to cultural norms.

His father worked long hours in construction, while his mother managed the household. Emotional expression was not commonly encouraged in his family. Carlos recalled, "We didn't really talk about our feelings. It was more about keeping things moving and making sure everyone was taken care of." He often felt the responsibility to set a good example for his younger siblings.

Carlos married his wife, Elena, at age 25. They have two children, both of whom have recently started their own families. Carlos described his marriage as stable but noted that he and Elena had grown somewhat distant emotionally. With the children gone, he felt a void and questioned his purpose beyond his roles as husband and father.

## Past Psychiatric History

Carlos had not previously engaged with mental health services and had no formal psychiatric diagnoses. He reported experiencing periods of low mood, irritability, and a sense of emptiness over the past few years. Cultural stigmas around mental health prevented him from seeking help earlier. He mentioned, "In my community, you handle your problems on your own. Going to therapy isn't something we usually do."

He denied any history of substance misuse and had never experimented with drugs, including psychedelics. His interest in psychedelics was sparked after attending a wellness seminar where the therapeutic potential of such substances was discussed.

## Case Formulation

Carlos's case involves a multifaceted interplay of cultural, psychological, and social factors. Psychologically, he is experiencing a midlife transition marked by feelings of stagnation and a search for renewed purpose. The departure of his children has led to an identity shift, leaving him questioning his roles and contributions.

Culturally, Carlos comes from a background in which seeking mental health support and discussing personal struggles is often stigmatized. This has contributed to his reluctance to express emotions and seek assistance, reinforcing his sense of isolation.

Socially, he faces challenges in his relationship with his wife due to emotional distancing and a lack of open communication. His interest in psychedelics represents a desire to break free from longstanding patterns and explore new dimensions of personal growth.

The primary targets for intervention included helping Carlos clarify his motivations for considering psychedelics, providing comprehensive psychoeducation about these substances, assisting him in evaluating potential risks and benefits, and supporting him in making a decision aligned with his values and life context.

## Course of Treatment

Over approximately nine months of weekly PHRI therapy, Carlos and I collaboratively explored his interest in psychedelics and his broader search for meaning and fulfillment.

## INITIAL PHASE:

Establishing a strong therapeutic alliance was essential. I provided a confidential and nonjudgmental space where Carlos felt comfortable sharing his thoughts and feelings. He was candid about his curiosity and apprehensions regarding psychedelics. Recognizing the importance of autonomy, I emphasized that my role was to support him in his decision-making process rather than to direct him toward any particular choice.

We began by exploring his motivations. Carlos expressed that he felt disconnected from himself and others and hoped that a psychedelic experience might provide insight or a sense of renewal. He was also concerned about potential legal issues, health risks, and the impact on his family and career.

## MIDDLE PHASE:

As therapy progressed, we delved deeper into Carlos's underlying feelings of dissatisfaction. I provided psychoeducation about psychedelics, discussing their history, therapeutic uses, legal status, and the importance of set and setting in shaping experiences. We reviewed potential risks, including psychological distress, adverse reactions, and the legal implications of using controlled substances.

Through reflective dialogues, Carlos began to articulate his desire for personal growth and reconnection with his passions. We utilized motivational interviewing techniques to help him weigh the pros and cons of pursuing a psychedelic experience. I encouraged him to consider how such an experience might align or conflict with his personal values, cultural beliefs, and professional responsibilities.

Carlos also explored alternative avenues for achieving his goals. He expressed interest in rekindling his love for music and art, activities he enjoyed in his youth but had set aside. Additionally, we discussed the possibility of engaging in mindfulness practices, such as meditation, to enhance self-awareness and emotional well-being.

## LATER PHASE:

In the latter stages of therapy, Carlos began to focus on actionable steps toward personal fulfillment without relying on psychedelics. He reconnected with his wife, initiating open conversations about their relationship and mutual desires for the future. Together, they decided to attend couples counseling to strengthen their bond.

Carlos also joined a community group for Latino men, which provided a supportive environment to share experiences and challenges. He resumed playing the guitar and started attending local art workshops, which reignited his creativity and joy.

Throughout this process, I continued to offer support and guidance, helping Carlos reflect on his experiences and feelings. He expressed appreciation for having a space to explore his thoughts without judgment or pressure.

## Outcome and Prognosis

By the end of our work together, Carlos decided not to pursue a psychedelic experience at this time. He stated, "I realized that what I was seeking was a deeper connection with myself and others, and there are many ways to achieve that." He felt empowered by making a decision that honored his values and responsibilities.

Carlos reported significant improvements in his mood and outlook on life. His relationship with Elena became more open and affectionate, and they planned activities to enjoy together. Engaging in creative pursuits and community involvement enhanced his sense of purpose and belonging.

The prognosis for Carlos is positive. He has demonstrated self-awareness, resilience, and a willingness to take proactive steps toward personal growth. Continued participation in meaningful activities and maintaining open communication within his relationships are recommended to support his ongoing well-being.

# Diagnostic Impressions (DSM-5)

- Adjustment Disorder with Mixed Anxiety and Depressed Mood (F43.23)

- No Substance Use Disorder

## Relevance to Broader Practice

Carlos's case highlights the importance of a client-centered approach in PHRI therapy, especially when clients are uncertain about engaging in psychedelic experiences. Key considerations include:

- **Nondirective Support:** Providing a space where clients can explore their thoughts and feelings without pressure allows them to arrive at decisions that are authentic and self-determined.

- **Psychoeducation:** Offering comprehensive information about psychedelics enables clients to make informed choices. This includes discussing potential benefits, risks, legal considerations, and alternative options.

- **Cultural Sensitivity:** Understanding the client's cultural background and values is crucial. In Carlos's case, acknowledging the stigmas around mental health in his community helped tailor the approach to his needs.

- **Exploring Underlying Needs:** Carlos's interest in psychedelics was a gateway to addressing deeper issues related to identity, purpose, and connection. Therapists can assist clients in identifying and pursuing these underlying desires through various means.

- **Ethical Practice:** Avoiding encouragement or discouragement of illegal activities while supporting the client's autonomy is essential. Upholding professional ethics ensures safe and responsible therapeutic engagement.

# References

Agin-Liebes, Gabrielle, Elizabeth M. Nielson, Michael Zingman, Katherine Kim, Alexandra Haas, Lindsey T. Owens, et al. 2023. "Reports of self-compassion and affect regulation in psilocybin-assisted therapy for alcohol use disorder: An interpretive phenomenological analysis." *Psychology of Addictive Behaviors* 38 (1): 101–113.

Amada, Nicole, and Jacob Shane. 2022. "Self-actualization and the integration of psychedelic experience: The mediating role of perceived benefits to narrative self-functioning." *Journal of Humanistic Psychology*: 00221678221099680.

Araújo, Ana Margarida, Félix Carvalho, Maria de Lourdes Bastos, Paula Guedes de Pinho, and Márcia Carvalho. 2015. "The hallucinogenic world of tryptamines: An updated review." *Archives of Toxicology* 89: 1151–1173.

Baggott, Matthew J. 2015. "Psychedelics and creativity: A review of the quantitative literature." *PeerJ PrePrints* 3: e1202v1.

Barnett, Brian S., Miranda Arakelian, David Beebe, Jared Ontko, Connor Riegal, Willie O. Siu, et al. 2024. "American psychiatrists' opinions about classic hallucinogens and their potential therapeutic applications: A 7-year follow-up survey." *Psychedelic Medicine* 2 (1): 1–9.

Barone, William, Jerome Beck, Michiko Mitsunaga-Whitten, and Phillip Perl. 2019. "Perceived benefits of MDMA-assisted psychotherapy beyond symptom reduction: Qualitative follow-up study of a clinical trial for individuals with treatment-resistant PTSD." *Journal of Psychoactive Drugs* 51 (2): 199–208.

Barrett, Frederick S., Matthew P. Bradstreet, Jeannie-Marie S. Leoutsakos, Matthew W. Johnson, and Roland R. Griffiths. 2016. "The Challenging Experience Questionnaire: Characterization of challenging experiences with psilocybin mushrooms." *Journal of Psychopharmacology* 30 (12): 1279–1295.

Barrett, Frederick S., Matthew W. Johnson, and Roland R. Griffiths. 2017. "Neuroticism is associated with challenging experiences with psilocybin mushrooms." *Personality and Individual Differences* 117: 155–160.

Basedow, Lukas A., and Sören Kuitunen-Paul. 2022. "Motives for the use of serotonergic psychedelics: A systematic review." *Drug and Alcohol Review* 41 (6): 1391–1403.

Bathje, Geoff J., Eric Majeski, and Mesphina Kudowor. 2022. "Psychedelic integration: An analysis of the concept and its practice." *Frontiers in Psychology* 13: 824077.

Becker, Bernard E. J. 2022. "Finding peace in the face of death: A depth-psychological inquiry into MDMA-assisted psychotherapy for anxiety associated with life-threatening illness." Pacifica Graduate Institute.

Bedi, Gillinder, David Hyman, and Harriet de Wit. 2010. "Is ecstasy an 'empathogen'? Effects of ±3, 4-methylenedioxymethamphetamine on prosocial feelings and identification of emotional states in others." *Biological Psychiatry* 68 (12): 1134–1140.

Belser, Alexander B., Gabrielle Agin-Liebes, T. Cody Swift, Sara Terrana, Neşe Devenot, Harris L. Friedman, et al. 2017. "Patient experiences of psilocybin-assisted psychotherapy: An interpretative phenomenological analysis." *Journal of Humanistic Psychology* 57 (4): 354–388.

Bershad, Anya K., Leah M. Mayo, Kathryne Van Hedger, Francis McGlone, Susannah C. Walker, and Harriet de Wit. 2019. "Effects of MDMA on attention to positive social cues and pleasantness of affective touch." *Neuropsychopharmacology* 44 (10): 1698–1705.

Blatchford, Emily, Stephen Bright, and Liam Engel. 2021. "Tripping over the other: Could psychedelics increase empathy?" *Journal of Psychedelic Studies* 4 (3): 163–170.

Bonson, Katherine R. 2012. "Hallucinogenic Drugs." In *eLS*, edited by Ltd John Wiley & Sons.

Bouso, José Carlos, Rick Doblin, Magí Farré, Miguel Ángel Alcázar, and Gregorio Gómez-Jarabo. 2008. "MDMA-assisted psychotherapy using low doses in a small sample of women with chronic posttraumatic stress disorder." *Journal of Psychoactive Drugs* 40 (3): 225–236.

Bouso, José Carlos, and Jordi Riba. 2014. "Ayahuasca and the treatment of drug addiction." In *The Therapeutic Use of Ayahuasca*, edited by Beatriz Caiuby Labate and Clancy Cavnar, 95–109. Berlin, Heidelberg: Springer Berlin Heidelberg.

Brown, Thomas Kingsley, and Kenneth Alper. 2018. "Treatment of opioid use disorder with ibogaine: Detoxification and drug use outcomes." *The American Journal of Drug and Alcohol Abuse* 44 (1): 24–36.

Buchborn, Tobias, Hannes S. Kettner, Laura Kärtner, and Marcus W. Meinhardt. 2023. "The ego in psychedelic drug action—ego defenses, ego boundaries, and the therapeutic role of regression." *Frontiers in Neuroscience* 17: 1232459.

Cameron, Lindsay P., Joseph Benetatos, Vern Lewis, Emma M. Bonniwell, Alaina M. Jaster, Rafael Moliner, et al. 2023. "Beyond the 5-HT2A receptor: Classic and nonclassic targets in psychedelic drug action." *Journal of Neuroscience* 43 (45): 7472–7482.

Campo, William M. 2022. "Psychedelic use and psychological flexibility: The role of decentering, mystical experiences, ego-dissolution, and insight." *CUNY Academic Works*, City University of New York.

Campo, William M, and Ann Marie Yali. 2024. "Psychedelic use and psychological flexibility: The role of meaningful intention and decentering." *Journal of Psychedelic Studies*: 2559–9283.

Carbonaro, T. M., M. P. Bradstreet, F. S. Barrett, K. A. MacLean, R. Jesse, M. W. Johnson, et al. 2016. "Survey study of challenging experiences after ingesting psilocybin mushrooms: Acute and enduring positive and negative consequences." *Journal of Psychopharmacology* 30 (12): 1268–1278.

Carbonaro, Theresa M., Matthew W. Johnson, Ethan Hurwitz, and Roland R. Griffiths. 2018. "Double-blind comparison of the two hallucinogens psilocybin and dextromethorphan: Similarities and differences in subjective experiences." *Psychopharmacology* 235 (2): 521–534.

Carhart-Harris, Robin L., Mark Bolstridge, James Rucker, Camilla M. J. Day, David Erritzoe, Mendel Kaelen, et al. 2016. "Psilocybin with psychological support for treatment-resistant depression: An open-label feasibility study." *The Lancet Psychiatry* 3 (7): 619–627.

Carod-Artal, F. J. 2015. "Hallucinogenic drugs in pre-Columbian Mesoamerican cultures." *Neurología (English Edition)* 30 (1): 42–49.

Colloca, Luana, Sina Nikayin, and Gerard Sanacora. 2023. "The intricate interaction between expectations and therapeutic outcomes of psychedelic agents." *JAMA Psychiatry* 80 (9): 867–868.

Connor, Jason P., Daniel Stjepanović, Bernard Le Foll, Eva Hoch, Alan J. Budney, and Wayne D. Hall. 2021. "Cannabis use and cannabis use disorder." *Nature Reviews Disease Primers* 7 (1): 16.

Costa, Miguel Ângelo. 2023. "A dose of creativity: An integrative review of the effects of serotonergic psychedelics on creativity." *Journal of Psychoactive Drugs* 55 (3): 299–309.

Cowley-Court, Tessa, Richard Chenhall, Jerome Sarris, José Carlos Bouso, Luís Fernando Tófoli, Emérita Sátiro Opaleye, et al. 2023. "Life after ayahuasca: A qualitative analysis of the psychedelic integration experiences of 1630 ayahuasca drinkers from a global survey." *Psychoactives* 2 (2): 201–221.

Danforth, Alicia L., Charles S. Grob, Christopher Struble, Allison A. Feduccia, Nick Walker, Lisa Jerome, et al. 2018. "Reduction in social anxiety after MDMA-assisted psychotherapy with autistic adults: A randomized, double-blind, placebo-controlled pilot study." *Psychopharmacology* 235 (11): 3137–3148.

de la Fuente Revenga, Mario, Alaina M. Jaster, John McGinn, Gabriella Silva, Somdatta Saha, and Javier González-Maeso. 2022. "Tolerance and cross-tolerance among psychedelic and nonpsychedelic 5-HT2A receptor agonists in mice." *ACS Chemical Neuroscience* 13 (16): 2436–2448.

Denomme, Nicholas, and Boris D. Heifets. 2024. "Ketamine, the first associative anesthetic? Some considerations on classifying psychedelics, entactogens, and dissociatives." *American Journal of Psychiatry* 181 (9): 784–786.

"Dextromethorphan." 2006. In *Meyler's Side Effects of Drugs: The International Encyclopedia of Adverse Drug Reactions and Interactions (Fifteenth Edition),* edited by J. K. Aronson, 1088–1092. Amsterdam: Elsevier.

Dominici, Paul, Kathryn Kopec, Rashmi Manur, Abdullah Khalid, Kathia Damiron, and Adam Rowden. 2015. "Phencyclidine intoxication case series study." *Journal of Medical Toxicology* 11: 321–325.

Dunn, H., J. Freeman, and M. Dochniak. 2023. "Psilocybin-based breakthroughs in natural medicine." *Case Rep Rev.* 3 (1): 1–15.

Dupuis, David. 2022. "The socialization of hallucinations: cultural priors, social interactions, and contextual factors in the use of psychedelics." *Transcultural Psychiatry* 59 (5): 625–637.

Elmer, Timon, Tanya K. Vannoy, Erich Studerus, and Sonja Lyubomirsky. 2024. "Subjective long-term emotional and social effects of recreational MDMA use: The role of setting and intentions." *Scientific Reports* 14 (1): 3434.

Evans, Jules, Oliver C. Robinson, Eirini Ketzitzidou Argyri, Shayam Suseelan, Ashleigh Murphy-Beiner, Rosalind McAlpine, et al. 2023. "Extended difficulties following the use of psychedelic drugs: A mixed methods study." *Plos one* 18 (10): e0293349.

Fattore, Liana, Alessandro Piva, Mary Tresa Zanda, Guido Fumagalli, and Cristiano Chiamulera. 2018. "Psychedelics and reconsolidation of traumatic and appetitive maladaptive memories: Focus on cannabinoids and ketamine." *Psychopharmacology* 235: 433–445.

Feduccia, Allison A., Lisa Jerome, Berra Yazar-Klosinski, Amy Emerson, Michael C. Mithoefer, and Rick Doblin. 2019. "Breakthrough for trauma treatment: Safety and efficacy of MDMA-assisted psychotherapy compared to paroxetine and sertraline." *Frontiers in Psychiatry* 10: 650.

Fischman, Lawrence G. 2019. "Seeing without self: Discovering new meaning with psychedelic-assisted psychotherapy." *Neuropsychoanalysis* 21 (2): 53–78.

Garcia-Romeu, Albert, Roland R. Griffiths, and Matthew W. Johnson. 2014. "Psilocybin-occasioned mystical experiences in the treatment of tobacco addiction." *Current Drug Abuse Reviews* 7 (3): 157–164.

Gearin, Alex K. 2016. "Good mother nature: Ayahuasca neoshamanism as cultural critique in Australia." In *The World Ayahuasca Diaspora*, 123–142. Routledge.

Gearin, Alex K. 2022. "Primitivist medicine and capitalist anxieties in ayahuasca tourism Peru." *Journal of the Royal Anthropological Institute* 28 (2): 496–515.

George, E., and L. Engel. 1980. "The clinical application of the biopsychosocial model." *American Journal of Psychiatry* 137 (5): 535–544.

Gershman, Jennifer A., and Andrea D. Fass. 2013. "Dextromethorphan abuse: A literature review." *Journal of Pharmacy Technology* 29 (2): 66–71.

Gezon, Lisa L. 2024. "Community-based psychedelic integration and social efficacy: An ethnographic study in the Southeastern United States." *Journal of Psychedelic Studies*.

Golden, Tasha L., Susan Magsamen, Clara C. Sandu, Shuyang Lin, Grace Marie Roebuck, Kathy M. Shi, et al. 2022. "Effects of setting on psychedelic experiences, therapies, and outcomes: A rapid scoping review of the literature." *Disruptive Psychopharmacology*: 35–70.

Goldy, Sean P., Peter S. Hendricks, Dacher Keltner, and David B. Yaden. 2024. "Considering distinct positive emotions in psychedelic science." *International Review of Psychiatry*: 1–12.

Gorman, Ingmar, Alexander B. Belser, Lisa Jerome, Colin Hennigan, Ben Shechet, Scott Hamilton, et al. 2020. "Posttraumatic growth after MDMA-assisted psychotherapy for posttraumatic stress disorder." *Journal of Traumatic Stress* 33 (2): 161–170.

Gorman, Ingmar, Elizabeth M. Nielson, Aja Molinar, Ksenia Cassidy, and Jonathan Sabbagh. 2021. "Psychedelic harm reduction and integration: A transtheoretical model for clinical practice." *Frontiers in Psychology* 12.

Gouzoulis-Mayfrank, Euphrosyne, Leo Hermle, Bernhard Thelen, and Henning Sass. 1998. "History, rationale and potential of human experimental hallucinogenic drug research in psychiatry." *Pharmacopsychiatry* 31 (S2): 63–68.

Greń, Jakub, Ingmar Gorman, Anastasia Ruban, Filip Tylš, Snehal Bhatt, and Marc Aixalà. 2023a. "Call for evidence-based psychedelic integration." *Experimental and Clinical Psychopharmacology* 32 (2): 129-135.

Greń, Jakub, Filip Tylš, Michał Lasocik, and Csaba Kiraly. 2023b. "Back from the rabbit hole: Theoretical considerations and practical guidelines on psychedelic integration for mental health specialists." *Frontiers in Psychology* 14: 1054692.

Grob, Charles S., Dennis J. McKenna, James C. Callaway, Glacus S. Brito, Edison S. Neves, Guilherme Oberlaender, et al. 1996. "Human psychopharmacology of hoasca, a plant hallucinogen used in ritual context in Brazil." *The Journal of Nervous and Mental Disease* 184 (2): 86–94.

Guss, Jeffrey. 2022. "A psychoanalytic perspective on psychedelic experience." *Psychoanalytic Dialogues* 32 (5): 452–468.

Haijen, Eline C. H. M., Mendel Kaelen, Leor Roseman, Christopher Timmermann, Hannes Kettner, Suzanne Russ, et al. 2018. "Predicting responses to psychedelics: A prospective study." *Frontiers in Pharmacology* 9.

Halberstadt, Adam L. 2015. "Recent advances in the neuropsychopharmacology of serotonergic hallucinogens." *Behavioural Brain Research* 277: 99–120.

Hall, Wayne. 2022. "Why was early therapeutic research on psychedelic drugs abandoned?" *Psychological Medicine* 52 (1): 26–31.

Halpern, John H., Arturo G. Lerner, and Torsten Passie. 2016. "A review of hallucinogen persisting perception disorder (HPPD) and an exploratory study of subjects claiming symptoms of HPPD." In *Behavioral Neurobiology of Psychedelic Drugs*, 333–360. Springer.

Hartogsohn, Ido. 2018. "The meaning-enhancing properties of psychedelics and their mediator role in psychedelic therapy, spirituality, and creativity." *Frontiers in Neuroscience* 12: 129.

———. 2020. *American Trip: Set, Setting, and the Psychedelic Experience in the Twentieth Century*. MIT Press.

Hayes, Steven C., and Heather Pierson. 2005. *Acceptance and Commitment Therapy*. Springer.

Healy, C. J., Kellie Ann Lee, and Wendy D'Andrea. 2021. "Using psychedelics with therapeutic intent is associated with lower shame and complex trauma symptoms in adults with histories of child maltreatment." *Chronic Stress* 5: 24705470211029881.

Hipólito, Inês, Jonas Mago, Fernando E. Rosas, and Robin Carhart-Harris. 2023. "Pattern breaking: A complex systems approach to psychedelic medicine." *Neuroscience of Consciousness* 2023 (1): niad017.

Holas, Paweł, and Justyna Kamińska. 2023. "Mindfulness meditation and psychedelics: Potential synergies and commonalities." *Pharmacological Reports* 75 (6): 1398–1409.

Huang, Ming-Chyi, and Shih-Ku Lin. 2020. "Ketamine abuse: Past and present." *Ketamine: From Abused Drug to Rapid-Acting Antidepressant:* 1–14. Springer.

Hysek, Cédric M., Yasmin Schmid, Linda D. Simmler, Gregor Domes, Markus Heinrichs, Christoph Eisenegger, et al. 2014. "MDMA enhances emotional empathy and prosocial behavior." *Social Cognitive and Affective Neuroscience* 9 (11): 1645-1652.

"Interview with Dr. Stanislav Grof." 2007. *Moscow Psychotherapeutic Journal.* https://stangrof.com/images/joomgallery/interviews/PDF/Moscow-Journal-Interview_Grof.pdf. Accessed 10/12/24.

Johnson, Matthew W., Katherine A. MacLean, Chad J. Reissig, Thomas E. Prisinzano, and Roland R. Griffiths. 2011. "Human psychopharmacology and dose-effects of salvinorin A, a kappa opioid agonist hallucinogen present in the plant Salvia divinorum." *Drug and Alcohol Dependence* 115 (1): 150–155.

Johnstad, Petter Grahl. 2021. "Day trip to hell: A mixed methods study of challenging psychedelic experiences." *Journal of Psychedelic Studies* 5 (2): 114–127.

Kanter, Jonathan W., Rachel C. Manos, William M. Bowe, David E. Baruch, Andrew M. Busch, and Laura C. Rusch. 2010. "What is behavioral activation?: A review of the empirical literature." *Clinical psychology review* 30 (6): 608–620.

Katzman, Jessica. 2018. "Rapid depression remission and the 'therapeutic bends.'" *Healing Realms*, August 30. https://www.healingrealms.com/blog/therapeuticbends.

Kavenská, Veronika, and Hana Simonová. 2015. "Ayahuasca tourism: Participants in shamanic rituals and their personality styles, motivation, benefits and risks." *Journal of Psychoactive Drugs* 47 (5): 351–359.

Kałużna, Ada, Marco Schlosser, Emily Gulliksen Craste, Jack Stroud, and James Cooke. 2022. "Being no one, being One: The role of ego-dissolution and connectedness in the therapeutic effects of psychedelic experience." *Journal of Psychedelic Studies.* 6 (2): 111–136

Ko, Kwonmok, Emma I. Kopra, Anthony J. Cleare, and James J. Rucker. 2023. "Psychedelic therapy for depressive symptoms: A systematic review and meta-analysis." *Journal of Affective Disorders* 322: 194–204.

Koretz, Zevi B. 2022. "Music Therapy Improvisation in the Integration of Psychedelic Therapy Experiences: A Process and Framework." Drexel University.

Kuc, Joanna, Hannes Kettner, Fernando Rosas, David Erritzoe, Eline Haijen, Mendel Kaelen, et al. 2022. "Psychedelic experience dose-dependently modulated by cannabis: Results of a prospective online survey." *Psychopharmacology* 239 (5): 1425–1440.

Kähönen, Juuso. 2023. "Psychedelic unselfing: Self-transcendence and change of values in psychedelic experiences." *Frontiers in Psychology* 14: 1104627.

Lee, Martin A., and Bruce Shlain. 1992. *Acid Dreams: The Complete Social History of LSD: The CIA, The Sixties, and Beyond.* Grove Press.

Letheby, Chris, and Philip Gerrans. 2017. "Self unbound: Ego dissolution in psychedelic experience." *Neuroscience of Consciousness* 2017 (1): nix016.

Litjens, Ruud P. W., and Tibor M. Brunt. 2016. "How toxic is ibogaine?" *Clinical Toxicology* 54 (4): 297–302.

Lutkajtis, Anna, and Jules Evans. 2023. "Psychedelic integration challenges: Participant experiences after a psilocybin truffle retreat in the Netherlands." *Journal of Psychedelic Studies* 6 (3): 211–221.

MacLean, K. A., M. W. Johnson, and R. R. Griffiths. 2011. "Mystical experiences occasioned by the hallucinogen psilocybin lead to increases in the personality domain of openness." *Journal of Psychopharmacology* 25 (11): 1453–1461.

Mantegani, Sergio, Enzo Brambilla, and Mario Varasi. 1999. "Ergoline derivatives: Receptor affinity and selectivity." *Il Farmaco* 54 (5): 288–296.

McCartney, A. M., H. T. McGovern, and Alexander De Foe. 2023. "Predictors of psychedelic experience: A thematic analysis." *Journal of Psychoactive Drugs* 55 (4): 411–419.

McGovern, H. T., H. J. Grimmer, M. K. Doss, B. T. Hutchinson, C. Timmermann, A. Lyon, et al. 2024. "An integrated theory of false insights and beliefs under psychedelics." *Communications Psychology* 2 (1): 69.

McGuire, Amy L., I. Glenn Cohen, Dominic Sisti, Matthew Baggott, Yuria Celidwen, Neşe Devenot, et al. 2024. "Developing an ethics and policy framework for psychedelic clinical care: A consensus statement." *JAMA Network Open* 7 (6): e2414650–e2414650.

McMillan, Riccardo Miceli. 2021. "Prescribing meaning: Hedonistic perspectives on the therapeutic use of psychedelic-assisted meaning enhancement." *Journal of Medical Ethics* 47 (10): 701–705.

Metzner, R., G. Litwin, and G. M. Weil. 1965. "The relation of expectation and mood to psilocybin reactions: A questionnaire study." *Psychedelic Review* 5, 3–39.

Miller, Christopher W. T. 2024. "The way of O: Phenomenology of psychedelic use and the path to ultimate reality." *Psychodynamic Practice*: 1–20.

Mitchell, Jennifer M., Michael Bogenschutz, Alia Lilienstein, Charlotte Harrison, Sarah Kleiman, Kelly Parker-Guilbert, et al. 2023. "MDMA-assisted therapy for severe PTSD: A randomized, double-blind, placebo-controlled phase 3 study." *Focus* 21 (3): 315–328.

Mithoefer, M. C., Mark T. Wagner, Ann T. Mithoefer, Lisa Jerome, Scott F. Martin, Berra Yazar-Klosinski, et al. 2013. "Durability of improvement in post-traumatic stress disorder symptoms and absence of harmful effects or drug dependency after 3, 4-methylenedioxymetham phetamine-assisted psychotherapy: A prospective long-term follow-up study." *Journal of Psychopharmacology* 27 (1): 28–39.

Mithoefer, M. 2013. "MDMA-assisted psychotherapy: How different is it from other psychotherapy?" *MAPS Bulletin Special Edition* Spring: 10–14.

Mograbi, Daniel C., Rafael Rodrigues, Bheatrix Bienemann, and Jonathan Huntley. 2024. "Brain networks, neurotransmitters and psychedelics: Towards a neurochemistry of self-awareness." *Current Neurology and Neuroscience Reports* 24 (8): 323–340.

Mollaahmetoglu, O. Merve, Johanna Keeler, Katherine J. Ashbullby, Eirini Ketzitzidou-Argyri, Meryem Grabski, and Celia J. A. Morgan. 2021. "'This is something that changed my life': A qualitative study of patients' experiences in a clinical trial of ketamine treatment for alcohol use disorders." *Frontiers in Psychiatry* 12: 695335.

Moreno, F. A., C. B. Wiegand, E. K. Taitano, and P. L. Delgado. 2006. "Safety, tolerability, and efficacy of psilocybin in 9 patients with obsessive-compulsive disorder." *Journal of Clinical Psychiatry* 67 (11): 1735–40.

Muttoni, Silvia, Maddalena Ardissino, and Christopher John. 2019. "Classical psychedelics for the treatment of depression and anxiety: A systematic review." *Journal of Affective Disorders* 258: 11–24.

Móró, Levente, Katalin Simon, Imre Bárd, and József Rácz. 2011. "Voice of the psychonauts: Coping, life purpose, and spirituality in psychedelic drug users." *Journal of Psychoactive Drugs* 43 (3): 188–198.

Müller, Felix, Elias Kraus, Friederike Holze, Anna Becker, Laura Ley, Yasmin Schmid, et al. 2022. "Flashback phenomena after administration of LSD and psilocybin in controlled studies with healthy participants." *Psychopharmacology* 239 (6): 1933–1943.

Nicholas, Christopher R., Julie B. Wang, Allison Coker, Jennifer M. Mitchell, Sukhpreet S. Klaire, Berra Yazar-Klosinski, et al. 2022. "The effects of MDMA-assisted therapy on alcohol and substance use in a phase 3 trial for treatment of severe PTSD." *Drug and Alcohol Dependence* 233: 109356.

Nichols, David E. 1981. "Structure-activity relationships of phenethylamine hallucinogens." *Journal of Pharmaceutical Sciences* 70 (8): 839–849.

———. 2022. "Entactogens: How the name for a novel class of psychoactive agents originated." *Frontiers in Psychiatry* 13: 863088.

Nygart, Victoria Amalie, Lis Marie Pommerencke, Eline Haijen, Hannes Kettner, Mendel Kaelen, Erik Lykke Mortensen, et al. 2022. "Antidepressant effects of a psychedelic experience in a large prospective naturalistic sample." *Journal of Psychopharmacology* 36 (8): 932–942.

O'Donnell, Kelley C., Lauren Okano, Michael Alpert, Christopher R. Nicholas, Chantelle Thomas, Bruce Poulter, et al. 2024. "The conceptual framework for the therapeutic approach used in phase 3 trials of MDMA-AT for PTSD." *Frontiers in Psychiatry* 15.

Paleos, C. Alexander. 2016. "Hallucinogens and Dissociative Drugs." *Pocket Guide to Addiction Assessment and Treatment*: 127.

Palhano-Fontes, Fernanda, Bruno Lobão Soares, Nicole Leite Galvão-Coelho, Emerson Arcoverde, and Draulio B. Araujo. 2022. "Ayahuasca for the Treatment of Depression." In *Disruptive Psychopharmacology*, edited by Frederick S. Barrett and Katrin H. Preller, 113–124. Cham: Springer International Publishing.

Pan, Wei, and Haiyan Bai. 2009. "A multivariate approach to a meta-analytic review of the effectiveness of the D.A.R.E. program." *International Journal of Environmental Research and Public Health* 6 (1): 267–277.

Passie, Torsten. 2023. *The History of MDMA*. Oxford University Press.

Patrick, M. E., R. A. Miech, L. D. Johnston, and P. M. O'Malley. 2023. "Monitoring the Future Panel Study annual report: National data on substance use among adults ages 19 to 60, 1976–2022." Monitoring the Future Monograph Series. University of Michigan Institute for Social Research, Ann Arbor, MI.

Pestana, Jani, Franca Beccaria, and Enrico Petrilli. 2021. "Psychedelic substance use in the Reddit psychonaut community: A qualitative study on motives and modalities." *Drugs and Alcohol Today* 21 (2): 112–123.

Pleet, Mollie M., Joshua White, Joseph A. Zamaria, and Rachel Yehuda. 2023. "Reducing the harms of nonclinical psychedelics use through a peer-support telephone helpline." *Psychedelic Medicine* 1 (2): 69–73.

Prochaska, James O., and John C. Norcross. 2001. "Stages of change." *Psychotherapy: Theory, Research, Practice, Training* 38 (4): 443.

Reissig, Chad J., Lawrence P. Carter, Matthew W. Johnson, Miriam Z. Mintzer, Margaret A. Klinedinst, and Roland R. Griffiths. 2012. "High doses of dextromethorphan, an NMDA antagonist, produce effects similar to classic hallucinogens." *Psychopharmacology* 223 (1): 1–15.

Riedlinger, June E. 1985. "The scheduling of MDMA: A pharmacist's perspective." *Journal of Psychoactive Drugs* 17 (3): 167–171.

Rivera-Illanes, D., and G. Recabarren-Gajardo. 2024. "Classics in chemical neuroscience: Muscimol." *ACS Chemical Neuroscience* 15 (18): 3257–3269.

Rosenbaum, Dennis P., and Gordon S. Hanson. 1998. "Assessing the effects of school-based drug education: A six-year multilevel analysis of Project D.A.R.E." *Journal of Research in Crime and Delinquency* 35 (4): 381–412.

Ross, S., A. Bossis, J. Guss, G. Agin-Liebes, T. Malone, B. Cohen, et al. 2016. "Rapid and sustained symptom reduction following psilocybin treatment for anxiety and depression in patients with life-threatening cancer: A randomized controlled trial." *Journal of Psychopharmacology* 30 (12): 1165–1180.

Russ, Suzanne L., Robin L. Carhart-Harris, Geoffrey Maruyama, and Melody S. Elliott. 2019. "States and traits related to the quality and consequences of psychedelic experiences." *Psychology of Consciousness: Theory, Research, and Practice* 6 (1): 1–21.

Samorini, Giorgio. 2019. "The oldest archeological data evidencing the relationship of Homo sapiens with psychoactive plants: A worldwide overview." *Journal of Psychedelic Studies* 3 (2): 63–80.

Sayalı, Ceyda, and Frederick S. Barrett. 2023. "The costs and benefits of psychedelics on cognition and mood." *Neuron* 111 (5): 614–630.

Schenberg, E. E., M. A. de Castro Comis, B. R. Chaves, and D. X. da Silveira. 2014. "Treating drug dependence with the aid of ibogaine: A retrospective study." *Journal of Psychopharmacology* 28 (11).

Shulgin, Alexander Theodore, and Ann Shulgin. 1991. *PIHKAL: A chemical love story.* Vol. 963009605. Berkeley, CA: Transform Press.

Skiles, Zachary, James R. Dixon, Dan Friedrich, Donny Reed, and Christopher S. Stauffer. 2023. "Peer support and psychedelics." *Journal of Military, Veteran and Family Health* 9 (5): 80–87.

Stocker, Kurt, and Matthias E. Liechti. 2024. "Methylenedioxymethamphetamine is a connectogen with empathogenic, entactogenic, and still further connective properties: It is time to reconcile 'the great entactogen–empathogen debate'." *Journal of Psychopharmacology* 38 (8): 685–689.

Strassman, R. 1995. "Hallucinogenic drugs in psychiatric research and treatment perspectives and prospects." *The Journal of Nervous and Mental Disease* 183 (3): 127–138.

Strassman, Rick J., Clifford R. Qualls, and Laura M. Berg. 1996. "Differential tolerance to biological and subjective effects of four closely spaced doses of N, N-dimethyltryptamine in humans." *Biological Psychiatry* 39 (9): 784–795.

Tatarsky, A., ed. 2007. *Harm Reduction Psychotherapy: A New Treatment for Drug and Alcohol Problems.* Jason Aronson, Inc.

Thiessen, Michelle S., Zach Walsh, Brian M. Bird, and Adele Lafrance. 2018. "Psychedelic use and intimate partner violence: The role of emotion regulation." *Journal of Psychopharmacology* 32 (7): 749–755.

Tulver, Kadi, Karl Kristjan Kaup, Ruben Laukkonen, and Jaan Aru. 2023. "Restructuring insight: An integrative review of insight in problem-solving, meditation, psychotherapy, delusions and psychedelics." *Consciousness and Cognition* 110: 103494.

Tupper, Kenneth W., and Beatriz C. Labate. 2014. "Ayahuasca, psychedelic studies, and health sciences: The politics of knowledge and inquiry into an Amazonian plant brew." *Current Drug Abuse Reviews* 7 (2): 71–80.

Turton, S., D. J. Nutt, and R. L. Carhart-Harris. 2014. "A qualitative report on the subjective experience of intravenous psilocybin administered in an fMRI environment." *Current Drug Abuse Reviews* 7 (2): 117–127.

Wagner, Mark T., Michael C. Mithoefer, Ann T. Mithoefer, Rebecca K. MacAulay, Lisa Jerome, Berra Yazar-Klosinski, et al. 2017. "Therapeutic effect of increased openness: Investigating mechanism of action in MDMA-assisted psychotherapy." *Journal of Psychopharmacology* 31 (8): 967–974.

Welwood, John. 1982. "The unfolding of experience: Psychotherapy and beyond." *Journal of Humanistic Psychology* 22 (1): 91–104.

———. 1984. "Principles of inner work: Psychological and spiritual." *The Journal of Transpersonal Psychology* 6 (1): 11.

Wheeler, Spencer W., and Natalie L. Dyer. 2020. "A systematic review of psychedelic-assisted psychotherapy for mental health: An evaluation of the current wave of research and suggestions for the future." *Psychology of Consciousness: Theory, Research, and Practice* 7 (3): 279.

Winkelman, M. 2005. "Drug tourism or spiritual healing? Ayahuasca seekers in amazonia." *Journal of Psychoactive Drugs* 37 (2): 209–218.

Woelfl, Timo, Cathrin Rohleder, Juliane K. Mueller, Bettina Lange, Anne Reuter, Anna Maria Schmidt, et al. 2020. "Effects of cannabidiol and delta-9-tetrahydrocannabinol on emotion, cognition, and attention: A double-blind, placebo-controlled, randomized experimental trial in healthy volunteers." *Frontiers in Psychiatry* 11: 576877.

Wolff, Max, Ricarda Evens, Lea J. Mertens, Michael Koslowski, Felix Betzler, Gerhard Gründer, et al. 2020. "Learning to let go: a cognitive-behavioral model of how psychedelic therapy promotes acceptance." *Frontiers in Psychiatry* 11: 5.

Yaden, David B., James B. Potash, and Roland R. Griffiths. 2022. "Preparing for the bursting of the psychedelic hype bubble." *JAMA Psychiatry* 79 (10): 943–944.

Zafar, Rayyan, Maxim Siegel, Rebecca Harding, Tommaso Barba, Claudio Agnorelli, Shayam Suseelan, et al. 2023. "Psychedelic therapy in the treatment of addiction: The past, present and future." *Frontiers in Psychiatry* 14: 1183740.

Zhou, Juan, Cassidy Scott, Ziba Rovei Miab, and Christian Lehmann. 2023. "Current approaches for the treatment of ketamine-induced cystitis." *Neurourology and Urodynamics* 42 (3): 680–689.

**Elizabeth Nielson, PhD,** is a psychologist, and cofounder of Fluence. She served as site coprincipal investigator of an FDA-approved Phase 3 clinical trial of MDMA-assisted therapy for post-traumatic stress disorder (PTSD), and worked on developing psychedelic therapies through conduct of additional FDA-approved trials of psychedelics for substance use problems and mood disorders. Nielson has published research on psychedelic therapies, psychedelic therapist training, and ethical considerations for the future of the field. Nielson has worked as an educator for clinicians for over a decade, and continues to create training programs to ensure the highest-quality care for psychedelic users.

**Ingmar Gorman, PhD,** is a psychologist, educator, and cofounder of Fluence. As site coprincipal investigator on FDA Phase 2 and Phase 3 clinical trials of MDMA-assisted therapy for PTSD, Gorman has been at the forefront of groundbreaking research in psychedelic-assisted psychotherapy. He has authored numerous publications on psychedelics, harm reduction, and integration therapy. Through his private practice and contributions to the field, Gorman continues to shape the future of mental health care.

# MORE BOOKS from
# NEW HARBINGER PUBLICATIONS

**BUDDHA'S BRAIN**

The Practical Neuroscience of
Happiness, Love, and Wisdom

**978-1648485602 / US $19.95**

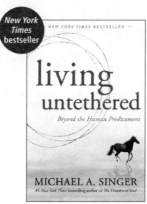

**LIVING UNTETHERED**

Beyond the Human Predicament

**978-1648480935 / US $18.95**

**THE HIGHLY SENSITIVE
PERSON'S GUIDE TO DEALING
WITH TOXIC PEOPLE**

How to Reclaim Your Power from
Narcissists and Other Manipulators

**978-1684035304 / US $20.95**

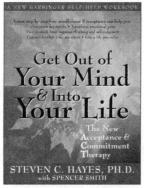

**GET OUT OF YOUR MIND
AND INTO YOUR LIFE**

The New Acceptance and
Commitment Therapy

**978-1572244252 / US $24.95**

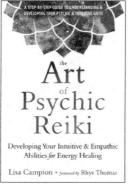

**THE ART OF PSYCHIC REIKI**

Developing Your Intuitive and
Empathic Abilities for Energy Healing

**978-1684031214 / US $19.95**

⊗ REVEAL PRESS
An Imprint of New Harbinger Publications

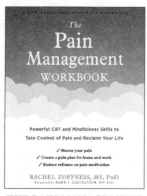

**THE PAIN MANAGEMENT
WORKBOOK**

Powerful CBT and Mindfulness
Skills to Take Control of Pain
and Reclaim Your Life

**978-1684036448 / US $24.95**

❀ new**harbinger**publications

1-800-748-6273 / newharbinger.com

(VISA, MC, AMEX / prices subject to change without notice)

Follow Us 📷 👍 ✖ ▶ 📌 in ♪ ⑥

Don't miss out on new books from New Harbinger.
Subscribe to our email list at **newharbinger.com/subscribe** ☌

# Did you know there are **free tools** you can download for this book?

Free tools are things like **worksheets**, **guided meditation exercises**, and **more** that will help you get the most out of your book.

You can download free tools for this book—whether you bought or borrowed it, in any format, from any source—from the New Harbinger website. All you need is a NewHarbinger.com account. Just use the URL provided in this book to view the free tools that are available for it. Then, click on the "download" button for the free tool you want, and follow the prompts that appear to log in to your NewHarbinger.com account and download the material.

You can also save the free tools for this book to your **Free Tools Library** so you can access them again anytime, just by logging in to your account! Just look for this button on the book's free tools page.

**+ Save this to my free tools library**

If you need help accessing or downloading free tools, visit **newharbinger.com/faq** or contact us at **customerservice@newharbinger.com**.